SIMON & SCHUSTER PAPERBACKS

NEW YORK LONDON TORONTO SYDNEY NEW DELHI

FINAL GIFTS

UNDERSTANDING THE SPECIAL AWARENESS, NEEDS, AND COMMUNICATIONS OF THE DYING

MAGGIE CALLANAN AND PATRICIA KELLEY

SIMON & SCHUSTER PAPERBACKS
A DIVISION OF SIMON & SCHUSTER, INC.
1230 AVENUE OF THE AMERICAS
NEW YORK, NY 10020

FIRST SIMON & SCHUSTER TRADE PAPERBACK EDITION FEBRUARY 2012

SIMON & SCHUSTER PAPERBACKS AND COLOPHON ARE
REGISTERED TRADEMARKS OF SIMON & SCHUSTER, INC.

FOR INFORMATION ABOUT SPECIAL DISCOUNTS FOR BULK
PURCHASES, PLEASE CONTACT SIMON & SCHUSTER SPECIAL SALES
AT 1-866-506-1949 OR BUSINESS@SIMONANDSCHUSTER.COM.

THE SIMON & SCHUSTER SPEAKERS BUREAU CAN BRING
AUTHORS TO YOUR LIVE EVENT. FOR MORE INFORMATION OR
TO BOOK AN EVENT, CONTACT THE SIMON & SCHUSTER
SPEAKERS BUREAU AT 1-866-248-3049 OR VISIT OUR WEBSITE
AT WWW.SIMONSPEAKERS.COM.

DESIGNED BY KAROLINA HARRIS

MANUFACTURED IN THE UNITED STATES OF AMERICA

10 9 8 7 6 5 4 3 2

THE LIBRARY OF CONGRESS HAS CATALOGED THE HARDCOVER
EDITION AS FOLLOWS:

CALLANAN, MAGGIE.
  FINAL GIFTS: UNDERSTANDING THE SPECIAL AWARENESS, NEEDS,
AND COMMUNICATIONS OF THE DYING / MAGGIE CALLANAN AND
PATRICIA KELLEY.
      P.   CM.
  INCLUDES BIBLIOGRAPHICAL REFERENCES.
  1. DEATH—PSYCHOLOGICAL ASPECTS. 2. TERMINALLY ILL—
PSYCHOLOGY. 3. TERMINALLY ILL—FAMILY RELATIONSHIPS.
4. DEATH—PSYCHOLOGICAL ASPECTS—CASE STUDIES.
5. TERMINALLY ILL—PSYCHOLOGY—CASE STUDIES.
6. TERMINALLY ILL—FAMILY RELATIONSHIPS—CASE STUDIES.
I. KELLEY, PATRICIA, 1945– . II. TITLE

ISBN 978-1-4516-6725-7
ISBN 978-1-4516-7729-4 (ebook)

ACKNOWLEDGMENTS

During the writing of this book, we have been fortunate to receive help and guidance from many talented people. Without the gentle encouragement and help from our first editor, Mary Boyken, this journey would never have started, nor would Nearing Death Awareness have been so named.

The professional journal *Nursing* was instrumental in this work by publishing our first article on this topic, and the National Hospice Organization encouraged us to share this information through their publications and conventions. Our thanks to both.

We also thank Wanda Wigfall-Williams for her advice and for introducing us to our agent, Gail Ross. Without exception, Gail has been our anchor, our guide, our advocate, and our friend.

We are grateful to our publisher, Ann Patty, and her staff, especially Fonda Duvanel, for their enthusiasm and assistance; and thank Michael Dolan for his valuable contribution as an editor for this book.

Maggie would like to acknowledge the talent, assistance, vision of clarity, and humor of Todd Pizer, without whom the final process of editing would have been much more difficult.

This book reflects not only our work, but that of many of our hospice colleagues over the years. Their dedication, enthusiasm, and remarkable capacity for caring makes them unique to all those who receive their care. Their support and contributions to this work have been invaluable to us, and as friends they have enriched our lives.

Most importantly, because this book could not have been written without them, we are grateful to the many dying people who were our finest teachers, and as such, gave us so many extraordinary gifts.

CONTENTS

III
NEARING DEATH AWARENESS:
WHAT I NEED FOR A PEACEFUL DEATH   125

FINAL

GIFTS

CHAPTER ONE

"IT'S TIME TO GET IN LINE."

LAURA

Joe paced anxiously—back and forth—at the foot of Laura's bed. There was an odd stillness in the room. He edged around the nurse's aide and the corner of the dresser so he could sit by his wife's side on the bed. Deeply concerned, he picked up her hand and began rubbing it.

"Laura, are you all right?" he asked. "Talk to me!"

She smiled dreamily and nodded, but said nothing. This upset Joe.

"Laura, it's me," he said. "Say something! I'm worried about you!"

"Joe, I'm okay," she whispered.

Joe looked to the nurse's aide, who responded with a look of uncertainty.

"Sweetheart, do you hurt?" he asked. "Do you need anything? Is something wrong? Darling, please tell me what it is?"

Laura smiled again, closed her eyes, and shook her head. Joe signaled for the aide to join him in the hall.

"What's wrong?" he asked. "She was fine this morning. A little weak, maybe, but fine. We had a cup of tea together."

The aide patted Joe's shoulder. "She just got this way. I don't know what's wrong. She's taken her medicines on schedule and she ate a little breakfast. Does she seem a bit confused to you?"

"It's hard to tell," Joe said. "She's not talking much. She seems real strange. We'd better call the nurse. I know something's wrong!" Joe nervously reached for the phone.

Someone you care about may be very ill, perhaps dying. There's so much to do—tests, hospitalizations, visits to doctors' offices. Sometimes there are two or three physicians to deal with—a surgeon, oncologist, radiologist, other specialists.

The medicine chest is jammed with partially used medicines—some bottles nearly full, others almost empty—as new and different ones are tried. Medical equipment seems to occupy every corner of the house. All the furniture has been rearranged, whether to allow a wheelchair to pass or to permit a fast trip to the bathroom.

Coping with terminal illness is more than hard work—it's all-consuming and creeps into every corner of your life. There are so many people to talk to, so many questions to ask, so much to do. The hopes and triumphs of new or different treatments can change quickly into fears and failures. It's an exhausting, emotional roller-coaster ride. It's like having an unwanted and uninvited stranger in your midst, who seems to take up more and more space.

A terminal illness doesn't belong only to the one who is sick—it affects family members, friends, neighbors, coworkers. Not unlike a still pond disturbed by a falling stone, an impending death sends ripples through all the relationships in the life of the dying. Each person involved has his or her own set of issues, fears, and questions.

Beyond coming to terms with the loss of someone we care about, we find ourselves with a jumble of conflicting emotions shaken loose by confronting human limitations and mortality: How can this be happening? I feel powerless—what can I do to help? I don't want to face this—what's it like to die? Is there anything after death? Why are the people around me behaving this way? I feel lost and helpless. What do I do? What do I say?

Is it possible to find anything positive in this devastating event? Can this remaining time be used to share treasured moments of living, while coping with the many losses death brings? Rather than dying on a continuum, can this person be helped to live until he or she dies? Can this be a time of personal growth for all involved?

Yes.

Laura had spent her life as a teacher, but when she retired and her first husband died, she decided to become a student again. This time her university was the world and she quenched her thirst for knowledge and new experiences by traveling—seeking new faces and new places.

In India she met Joe—a fellow traveler in her tour group. An enthusiastic widower of seventy-nine, he had an inviting twinkle in his eye and shared Laura's touring style—each lived out of a backpack, like the far younger vagabonds they encountered on the road. They were immediately drawn to each other, fell in love, returned home, and—much to the surprise of the grown children they both had—announced their engagement.

The wedding was small and charming, attended by their children and grandchildren. Laura wore a sari she'd bought in India and was given away by one of her grandsons. She'd chosen Robbie to do the honors because she wanted to feel a sense of connection with his mother—her daughter Susan, who'd died of breast cancer the year before at the age of forty-five.

Joe's best man was his son. After the ceremony, everyone feasted on Indian food served on Laura's treasured antique Russian china.

Laura sold her house and gave away much of her furniture; Joe moved out of the apartment he'd occupied since his first wife's death. They rented a one-bedroom apartment in a retirement complex, which was crammed with the belongings that once had filled their two large houses. It was a squeeze for them to pass each other in the narrow hallway, cluttered with cabinets, mirrors, storage shelves, and clocks from Joe's collection. But they were happy, and Laura was able to indulge her passion for gardening by working on the building's grounds.

Once settled, Joe and Laura returned to traveling—now as a twosome. The once-tedious aspects of the tourist life—baggage lines, ticket lines, customs lines, lines for planes and buses and trains—now were occasions to enjoy one another's company.

Joe was quite forgetful, so he relied heavily on Laura as an organizer and manager—roles she loved.

They had to cut short a trip to Mexico celebrating Laura's eighty-third birthday, when she came down with dysentery. Her condition persisted until she had to be hospitalized for dehydration. But X-rays showed a tumor in her colon, which when removed was found to be malignant. The cancer had already spread to Laura's liver and, considering her age, aggressive treatment wasn't recommended; the doctors said she had about six months to live.

Joe took this news badly, seeming to become more muddled than usual. Laura decided to spend her remaining time at home with Joe, who was eager to help in any way he could. They decided to call the hospice for help and support.

The next four months passed uneventfully. Laura's discomfort was minimal, and easily controlled with medications. Their families visited often, bringing meals or simply spending time with her. She and Joe would sit for hours paging through albums of photos from their trips and their younger days. These weren't always happy interludes; pictures of Susan as a healthy young woman always made Laura cry.

"Mothers aren't supposed to outlive their children," she'd say. "I miss her so much. It should have been me, not her."

However, Laura was stoic about her own situation, and did her best to maintain her social contacts and gracious manners. But her terminal diagnosis and increasing dependency were beginning to overwhelm Joe. His distress showed in his behavior. When Laura asked for a pain pill, he would dash off with great purpose, but distract himself along the way with a series of meaningless activities, and forget the medicine.

Laura's children dealt with this by hiring a home health aide, who wound up spending nearly as much time and energy helping Joe as she did Laura.

They managed quite well until the morning Laura's behavior

changed. She refused the bath that she usually enjoyed, and seemed distracted and distant. Joe was alarmed when he called our hospice.

I arrived to find him agitated and impatiently waiting for me at the apartment door.

"She's different today," he said. "She's looking at us—but through us—like we're not there."

Laura seemed restless and preoccupied, picking at the bed-covers and staring into space with a faraway look in her eyes. A quick physical check revealed no apparent reason for this change in her behavior.

"What's happening to you, Laura?" I asked. "Where have you been?"

"It's time to get in line," she said.

"Tell me more about the line," I said. "Is there anybody there you know?"

"Susan is in the line," Laura said, breaking into a radiant smile, but continuing to stare into space.

"How nice for you," I said. "Would you like to get in line? Can you tell me more?"

Laura became thoughtful, and sad. After a few moments she said, "But Joe can't go with me."

I sensed that she was feeling torn between going to be with the daughter she missed so terribly and staying with the husband who needed her so much.

"That must be a hard choice for you, Laura," I said. "Can we help Joe get ready for the time when you have to get in line?"

Laura visibly relaxed, and simply said, "Yes."

Joe was in the living room, surrounded by antique furniture and exotic souvenirs from their travels. Around him half a dozen clocks were ticking, each one set at a different time. I joined him on the sofa and told him about my conversation with Laura. He began to cry.

"I know this is hard for you, Joe," I said, handing him tissues. "What do you think Laura is telling us?"

"It sounds like she's dreaming about seeing Susan," Joe said. "Like maybe they'll be reunited."

"What else do you think she might be saying?"

"It sounds like she wishes I could go with her," he said. "But I can't—maybe she's worried about that."

"Is there any specific reason Laura might be worried about leaving you behind?"

"I depend on her a lot," he said. "I suppose she's worried about how I'll get along without her."

"Do you have plans for managing on your own?" I asked.

"Yes," he said. "I know I'm not as sharp as I used to be, so I'm going to move in with my son." Joe went on to describe in detail the arrangements he'd made.

"Your plans sound good," I said. "Does Laura know about them?"

Joe looked horrified. "You can't tell someone who's dying what you're going to do after they're gone!" he said.

I suggested that this might be exactly what Laura needed to hear, to ease her anguish about leaving him.

Joe hunched over, elbows on his knees, face hung in sadness.

"It's so hard to talk about this," he said. "I hate even thinking about it. It's just the worst thing I can imagine. . . ."

I let him continue to express his feelings and concerns for a while, then repeated my thoughts about Laura's needing reassurance that he understood what was happening to her. Joe would again lose focus, and I would gently remind him of what we were discussing. Several times he suddenly stood—as if to end the conversation—but seemed to realize there wasn't anywhere for him to go in the crowded room, and he would simply sit back down.

Finally, Joe was able to go into the bedroom, sit by Laura's side, and hold her hand. With tears streaming down his cheeks, he shared his plans and gave her permission to die.

"I hate that this is happening, but I know you have to go," he told her. "I'll bet you're worried about me, but I promise I'll be all right. Let me tell you about my plans, so you can rest easy."

Joe described what he would do after she died. He was going to spend winters with his youngest brother in Florida and summers with his son's family up North. Both homes had gardens;

Joe told Laura he'd work to keep them as beautiful as she would.

"And I'll do my best to remember all the kids' birthdays—your grandchildren's and mine!" he said, kissing his wife.

After that conversation, Laura's preoccupation and restlessness stopped. She became peaceful, and remained so until she died a few days later—with Joe tearfully holding her hand.

Comments like Laura's—"It's time to get in line"—are often heard when someone is near death. It's easy to label such comments as "confusion", and stop listening. Had he done so, Joe would have missed these important messages:

- I'm getting ready to die soon.
- I'll be reunited with Susan.
- I need to know that Joe understands and is prepared for my leaving.
- I need assurance that he'll be all right after I'm gone.

Joe's honest response eased Laura's pain—not physical pain but emotional and spiritual pain. After Joe explained his plans and said good-bye, she was able to live out her last days without anguish, having the information she needed to die peacefully.

Dying people often employ symbolic language that evokes their life experiences. Laura and Joe had met while traveling, and their lives had been full of ticket lines, baggage lines, and passport lines. With her comment, she was telling him she must now prepare for her next journey—one she couldn't take with him—by getting "in line with Susan."

Laura's final gifts to Joe were the realization that she was concerned about his welfare, that she was not alone in her dying and would be reunited with Susan.

After Laura's funeral, Joe said, "I know she'll be waiting for me when I die—the way Susan was waiting for her." His experience with Laura's death was already changing Joe's expectations about his own death.

. . .

You, too, can gain the insight and understanding you need to find something good in the sadness and pain of losing someone you care about. What you learn from this book—and from dying people—you can carry forward into the rest of your life.

We are not researchers or philosophers; we're nurses who choose to work with dying people. The material in this book has come directly from our finest teachers—our dying patients, who have taught us what dying is like for them while they are experiencing it. What we have learned is so exciting and positive that it has changed our lives, and we have written this book to share those messages with you.

We didn't set out to develop a new theory on the special communication by the dying—we simply listened, with our ears, with our hearts, and with open minds. We now invite you to open your minds and hearts to the positive, final messages of the dying.

I

NEARING DEATH AWARENESS: INTRODUCTION AND BACKGROUND

.

CHAPTER TWO

NEARING DEATH
AWARENESS:
AN INTRODUCTION

FINAL GIFTS is for everyone who has been or will ever be close to someone who is dying—for families and friends, for health-care workers, for dying people themselves. Those who are dying and those who care about them often have valuable gifts to offer one another. When someone you love is dying you may not see gifts, but only grief, pain, and loss. However, a dying person offers enlightening information and comfort, and in return those close at hand can help bring that person peace and recognition of life's meaning.

What we term "Nearing Death Awareness" is a special knowledge about—and sometimes a control over—the process of dying. Nearing Death Awareness reveals what dying is like, and what is needed in order to die peacefully; it develops in those who are dying slowly. The attempts of dying people to describe what they are experiencing may be missed, misunderstood, or ignored because the communication is obscure, unexpected, or expressed in symbolic language.

In the final hours, days, or weeks of life, dying people often make statements or gestures that seem to make no sense. Family members or friends may say, "Her mind is wandering," or "He doesn't know what's happening now." It's not unusual for an onlooker, however well-meaning, to speak of the dying person as "out of it" or "losing it" or "not quite right anymore." Health-care professionals, especially doctors and nurses, may label these apparently illogical expressions as "confusion" or "hallucination."

Family, friends, and professionals frequently respond with frustration or annoyance. They may try to humor the patient, sometimes behaving as if they're dealing with a child. They may try to stop the confusion with medication.

All of these responses serve only to distance dying people from those they trust, producing a sense of isolation and bewilderment. No matter what label is placed on their attempts to communicate, or which responses are tried, everyone stops really listening to the dying person.

There is another way.

By keeping open minds and by listening carefully to dying people, we can begin to understand messages they convey through symbol or suggestion. Often, we can decipher essential information and in the deciphering relieve a dying person's anxiety and distress. By trying to understand, and therefore participate more fully in the events of dying, families and friends can gain comfort, as well as important knowledge about what the experience of dying is like and what is needed to achieve a peaceful death. They can carry that new knowledge forward, finding continuing solace in it after the death of the person they loved, and as they face future deaths, including their own. By becoming more sensitive to the messages and needs of the dying, professionals can give better care and gain a greater sense of satisfaction.

After many years of working with dying people and after hundreds of experiences with their special type of communication, we have identified several recurring themes. These messages fall into two categories: attempts to describe what someone is experiencing while dying, and requests for something that a person needs for a peaceful death.

The experience of dying frequently includes glimpses of another world and those waiting in it. Although they provide few details, dying people speak with awe and wonder of the peace and beauty they see in this other place. They tell of talking with, or sensing the presence of, people whom we cannot see—perhaps people they have known and loved. They know, often without being told, that they are dying, and may even tell us when their deaths will occur.

Dying persons' requests are sometimes difficult to decipher. Their recognition of the importance of these needs, along with concern for family and friends, can cause the dying to control the time and circumstances of death until those needs are met. These requests often involve someone else; they may be for meetings or the healing of relationships.

Such messages have a universal familiarity. For centuries, many cultures have documented aspects of dying, taking note of altered states of consciousness, mystical interludes, and deathbed visions. Literature contains many descriptions of dying people seeing visions, usually interpreted as signs of impending death. Researchers have found sharp similarities among death-bed visions in radically differing cultures and societies.

Nearing Death Awareness often includes visions of loved ones or spiritual beings, although they don't necessarily signal death's imminence. Dying people may see and speak with religious fig-ures. They may feel warm, peaceful, and loved; some see a bright light or another place. Some review their lives and come to a more complete understanding of life's meaning. Realizing they are dying, they don't seem to feel fear; rather, they express concern for those who will be left behind.

In some ways this resembles the near-death experience, a phenomenon reported by people resuscitated after being clini-cally dead (that is, without heartbeat, breathing, blood pressure, or other signs of life). Researchers have documented how, after being revived, such people report remarkably similar events—traveling through a tunnel, seeing a bright light, meeting de-ceased relatives or friends, being in the presence of a supreme being, experiencing a life review, undergoing feelings of peace-fulness and relief of pain.

Out-of-body experiences (in which a person travels out of the physical body) can occur in such instances, but also may happen in other situations, especially in instances of great stress. Later, such travelers may report seeing things not visible from within their physical bodies. They may recount conversations that took place far away, or describe distant, even unknown places.

Nearing Death Awareness and near-death experiences are similar, but there are important distinctions. A near-death experience happens suddenly—as a result of drowning, heart attack, or traffic accident, for example—while Nearing Death Awareness develops in people dying slowly of progressive illnesses, such as cancer, AIDS, lung disease. For these people the process of leaving this world and experiencing a new one is more gradual. Rather than being in this world one moment, gone from it the next, then jerked back to life, the dying person remains inside the body, but at the same time becomes aware of a dimension that lies beyond. Rather than switching abruptly from one world to another, dying people apparently drift between the two. Instead of seeing their lives flash past, dying people seem to have more time to assess those lives and to determine what remains to be finished before they die.

With Nearing Death Awareness people don't appear dead; they may undergo no visible or unusual physical change. They still have pulses and blood pressures, they continue to breathe; most important, they continue to communicate. They may attempt to describe being in two places at once, or somewhere in between. Their descriptions offer unique opportunities to enter that landscape, to participate by responding to their needs and wishes, and to learn what death is like for them—and, perhaps, what it will be like for us.

For several reasons, onlookers often miss or misunderstand the dying person's attempts to communicate about Nearing Death Awareness.

Health-care professionals and families may assume that what they're hearing and seeing is confusion—in medical terms, a mental state characterized by bewilderment or disorientation and inappropriate reactions to stimuli. Unfortunately, dying people are often labeled "confused" without adequate assessment. The truly confused patient may have dementia—an acquired, usually progressive disorder of the intellect, unconnected with normal dying. The patient may be delirious, possibly as a result of fever or as a reaction to a medicine. Confusion can result from a physiological condition such as too much calcium in the blood or too little oxygen in the brain. Some of these conditions can be treated or at least controlled.

Dying people who seem confused may not have these problems, and no matter what is causing the disorientation, a dying person's "confused" talk may be significant.

In dying people, bewilderment or disorientation may stem from the unfamiliar, unexpected experiences of dying. And, too often, the responses of those caring for dying people only add to that bewilderment.

Family members and caregivers may dismiss what they're hearing as a dying person's dreams or memories. The dreams of the dying may contain powerful messages, especially about strong feelings, but dying people know implicitly that Nearing Death Awareness experiences differ from dreams. Sometimes the dying person may begin to describe them by saying, "I had a dream, but it wasn't really a dream. . . ."

Those who have had near-death experiences often cannot put into words what they have seen or felt. After a grave heart attack, Carl Jung said, "It is impossible to convey the beauty and intensity . . ." A colleague of ours who had a near-death experience during a life-threatening complication following surgery had the same difficulty.

"I really can't think of words that say enough," she said. "The experience was so intense. I guess 'infinite' comes the closest."

"Is our language too finite to describe such an infinite experience?" we asked.

"Yes," she said. "That's it!"

Similarly, those in the midst of Nearing Death Awareness may lack words to describe the experience of dying, making their messages difficult to understand because they express them in symbolic language instead of straightforward descriptions.

Familiar expressions, gestures, or even objects are often used as potent metaphors. By analyzing these attempts at communication in the context of someone's life, we can better understand what the person is trying to tell us.

But if we don't expect such messages, we can miss them. Few of us expect a dying person to have anything new to teach. Overwhelmed by sadness or upset by the deterioration of someone they love, family and friends can overlook that person's messages. As distressing as it is to watch someone you love struggle with pain or nausea or extreme weight loss, it's harder to accept what appears to be that person's disorientation. The person seems to have become distant, a stranger. Those who categorize Nearing Death Awareness as "confusion" not only miss opportunities to learn from and assist the dying, they also add to families' and friends' discomfort.

Professionals adept at dealing with physical problems may not be as skilled at explaining the change in a dying person's mental and emotional state. They want to be of assistance, but don't know how. This can frustrate families already uncomfortable, even fearful, in the presence of someone dying. They don't know what to say, what to do, how to act.

Final Gifts offers information and suggestions to help you learn from a dying person, and in the process understand more about the experience of dying. You needn't be a nurse or doctor or have any medical training to help a dying friend or relative. In fact, the very closeness of kinship or friendship attunes family members and friends to the symbolic language and gestures that may accompany Nearing Death Awareness.

And it's important to note that, although many of the case studies in this book came from our work in hospice care, these experiences don't happen only to hospice patients. Some of those who described their experiences of Nearing Death Awareness with us were receiving care through home health agencies, some in hospitals, some in nursing homes. Some were patients; some were friends. The issue isn't setting or type of care but the importance of showing interest and concern, as well as willingness to listen and pay attention.

In reading *Final Gifts,* you will discover how to listen to a dying person, how to weigh gesture and meaning so as to avoid responses that alienate and frustrate. You will see how others have approached a death in their lives in ways that have brought comfort and peace, even joy. And you will gain a peace and comfort of your own, as well as a greater awareness of the power of dying.

CHAPTER THREE

BEGINNINGS

Those of us who work with dying patients and their families often are asked to explain what seems to be a somber and grueling choice of career. "How can you do it?" "Isn't it depressing?"

The truth is that our work brings tremendous satisfaction, fulfillment, and even joy. How is this possible? Part of the answer is that we have come to recognize the parallels between being born and dying—between entering this world and leaving it—and this understanding helps us to define our function and rewards.

As nurses who care for the dying, we see ourselves as the counterparts of birthing coaches or midwives, who assist in bringing life from the womb into the world. At the other end of life, we help to ease the transition from life through death to whatever exists beyond.

Our message to the patients and families with whom we work is "Let me tell you what we know about this process. Let's apply it to you and your individual qualities, needs, and relationships, and together we can make this experience the best it can be for you and your family."

In some cases we encountered the people you will read about in hospital or home-health-care settings; some material came from the personal experiences of others. But we developed much of the information during our years working with dying patients as hospice nurses.

Once, birth and death were home-centered everywhere, and they remain so in many countries still. But in some industrialized nations of the twentieth century, they were moved from the home to the hospital. Birth and death became medical procedures, managed by hospital personnel and protocol.

In childbirth, the job of mothers-to-be was to follow directions, right down to using whichever anesthetic or analgesic was deemed appropriate by the doctor. Fathers were banned from the delivery room, and family members were considered outsiders—even intruders—to whom information was fed bit by bit.

Many of the same restrictions apply to the dying patients, who may also experience the additional humiliation of being seen as the failures of medical science. Without realizing that they are doing it, medical staff often put dying patients in rooms as far as possible from nursing stations, and health-care workers seem slow to answer their call bells.

But there's been a change. In recent years, parents and baby have come to take precedence over institutional policy and technological demands. Birth is again being seen as part of life, not a matter of medical procedure. Pregnant women are now demanding and receiving all the information they want—and need—to understand pregnancy and delivery. They decide where to deliver, who will be on hand, and which method of pain relief, if any, they will use. Fathers and older children are part of childbirth education, and often participate in the birth itself, which may or may not involve a hospital and physician. Many women are choosing to deliver at home, assisted by a birthing coach or midwife. When birth does take place in a hospital, it often occurs in birthing suites decorated to be cozier and more homelike than the usual sterile delivery room.

This increased control and better access to information has led to a greater sense of comfort with the whole process of birthing. Family members present at delivery share a special bond with mother and child—a closeness born of sharing that powerful moment. The deeper their involvement and understanding, the likelier they are to come away with a sense of learning and growth.

Just so, the process of dying has begun to return to the "old-fashioned" way. Thanks to the rise of the hospice movement, the emphasis has shifted from professional providers of care and their tools to those most centrally involved—patient and informal caregiver, whether family or friend. As with childbirth, the care of the dying is now influenced as much as possible by those main players, who receive as much information as they want and need. Dying patients are seen less often as passive targets for diagnostic tests and painkillers, and more often as individuals with control over their living and dying.

Given the choice, most people prefer to die at home; most families prefer truthful reports on a terminal patient's condition. Though the idea of providing care at home for someone dying can be formidable and frightening, many families are able to handle it. With the proper training and support, they can learn the skills needed to keep a dying person comfortable—especially in light of advances in pain control that allow a layperson to administer medications that ease discomfort without drugging someone into a stupor. And, at the end, patients feel less isolated and fearful, while those present come away more comforted, knowing that they've participated as fully as possible in the death of someone they care about.

Though it can be grief- and stress-laden, death can occur in a context of completion and closure. After going through a death this way, many people say, "This may have been the hardest thing I've ever done, but I'm so glad I did it," or "The only thing that really helps me now that she's gone is that she knew, as I do, that I did everything I could for her."

Hospice is the main setting in which care of the dying has evolved into a natural, patient-centered approach. This special way of care is based on two principles: that dying people should be able to choose how they spend the time they have left, and that their remaining time should be as peaceful and comfortable as possible.

Hospice also helps family and friends get through this difficult life event in as positive a manner as possible. The many supportive but nontraditional relationships of today indicate that ties of blood or marriage are not necessarily the strongest for everyone. Our concept of family members—used throughout this book—includes whomever the patient chooses as such.

Most hospice patients spend their last days not in an institutional setting—such as a nursing home or hospital—but in their own homes, although inpatient care is available when necessary—in a hospice facility, a hospital, or a nursing home.

Regardless of size, shape, or affiliation, hospice is more than a place or a group of people; it's a concept of caring. Those of us who work in hospice see it not as a job but as a philosophy that has a profound effect on our lives as well as on the lives of those for whom we care.

The hospice movement is at once ancient and modern, an old form of comfort for travelers—now adapted as a philosophy of care, to ease the journey from life to death.

In medieval times, a hospice was a place where voyagers or pilgrims could stop for rest, food, shelter, or help when they were tired, sick, or dying. There were hundreds of hospices throughout Europe and along the routes to the Holy Land. In the early 1800s the Irish Sisters of Charity established several hospices in Ireland and England, and it was at one of them— St. Joseph's, in London—that a British physician, Dame Cicely Saunders, began the work that would lead to her developing the basis of the modern-day hospice movement.

In 1960, Dr. Saunders proposed a new way of caring for such patients—a hospice like those of the Middle Ages, but organized as a peaceful place "for the care of the dying on a metaphysical journey from this world to the next." Her approach combined loving, compassionate care with sophisticated medical intervention that emphasized palliative care (relief of symptoms) rather than curative care (treatments or procedures intended to stop or reverse an illness or condition). In 1967 in a London suburb, Dr. Saunders opened St. Christopher's Hospice, the seedling from which today's worldwide hospice movement grew.

"You matter because you are," Dr. Saunders told dying people. "You matter until the last moment of your life, and we will do all we can not only to help you die peacefully but also to live until you die."

At about the same time, the work and writings of Dr. Elisabeth Kübler-Ross, a psychiatrist in the United States, began to change our attitudes toward death and dying in a way that allowed the hospice movement to take root and flourish.

At a 1959 Yale University symposium, Dr. Kübler-Ross presented a paper describing how dying patients suffered, even in the finest medical facilities. Usually isolated from other patients, often heavily sedated—yet still in pain—the dying were rarely included in decisions about the procedures imposed on them. Endlessly tested to monitor the courses of their illnesses and treatments, they were often handled as bundles of physical symptoms, or simply as failures of the medical system. But lost in all this "expert treatment" was a human being with fears, questions, desires, needs, and rights. Dr. Kübler-Ross expanded on this theme in her 1961 book, *On Death and Dying*, which gave the public a new and different way of viewing the terminal patient.

Because the hospice movement is relatively new and the nurse's role in it differs greatly from that of a hospital nurse, many people have difficulty understanding the job. A hospice nurse is part of an interdisciplinary team—doctor, nurse, social worker, chaplain, and volunteers, with other specialists such as dieticians and physical or respiratory therapists brought in as needed—whose members play two key roles: care of the patient *and* care of the family. They teach family members and friends how to provide and manage a patient's care at home, as well as what to expect as the patient's condition changes. They also determine whether caregivers have the physical and emotional help needed to get through this rigorous task. After death, bereavement support is available to caregivers and family.

The evolution of home care has meant that many types of equipment and many functions once possible only in medical facilities—professional monitoring of patients' vital signs and delivery of intravenous pain medications, for example—can be provided at home. This lets patients remain in that least threatening, most comfortable setting, cared for by family members, who also have access to hospice workers at any hour of any day. Doctors and nurses are on call evenings, weekends, and holidays.

Hospice home-care nurses, although part of the team, spend much of their time working alone, managing the care of six to ten patients. A home visit lasts an hour or two; the frequency and length depend on how well patient and family are doing. At first the nurse comes two or three times a week, stopping by more often—sometimes daily—as death draws closer.

The hospice philosophy maintains that patients should get as much information as they want about the changes taking place in their bodies, about the probable courses of their diseases, and about the likely scenarios of their deaths. Nothing is forced on anyone; care is controlled not by professional convenience or practice, but by patients themselves.

Of course, in any terminal illness, there is much that can only be tempered—the speed and intensity with which the disease progresses, the degree of physical deterioration, the number and severity of symptoms. To balance against the perception that their bodies are out of control, hospice encourages patients to control their own medications, treatments, even site of death—and in maintaining some control, get the most out of the time left to them.

In hospice, symptom control aims to decrease suffering and increase comfort in four areas: physical, emotional, social, and spiritual. Physical discomfort can be excruciating, but with careful assessment and skilled treatment, it is often the easiest to manage. Pain can be relieved. Nausea can be quelled. Constipation can be eased. The other elements can be more elusive, and involve people other than the patient.

Illness causes emotional discomfort—depression, anger, anxiety, fear, or any one of the spectrum of feelings caused by death's approach. How is the patient handling these emotions? What kind of assistance does he or she need?

Terminal illness also causes social discomfort, upsetting the patient's relationships with others. Is a spouse or parent overwhelmed with sadness? Is a child upset, angry, or frightened by the changes in the dying person? Are friends pulling away because they don't know what to do or say? Does the patient or family feel rejected or abandoned?

Spiritual discomfort is the result of mortality's impact on patient and family. Is the patient asking himself whether his life has been worthwhile? Is she wondering what life has meant, what dying means? Is there life after death? And if so, what will it be like? For people who embrace religion, questions may arise about God or a supreme being—"How could He let this happen to me, to my family? Why does He allow such suffering?"—as well as doubts about a faith that until now has provided spiritual sustenance.

The comparative ease with which physical symptoms can be remedied isn't echoed in the other three areas of comfort. Emotional, social, and spiritual symptoms are not only more subtle and therefore more difficult to define and correct; they also can be complicated by a patient's personality and a family's lifestyle. Medicine has become highly specialized to focus with great expertise on a particular body system or illness. But patient and family exist as a unit—interacting and struggling together in what can become a perplexing maze of distress and anxiety.

The solution to this maze requires attentiveness and willingness to listen and understand. Dying people communicate in wondrous but sometimes strange ways, and it takes persistence and insight to catch and decipher their messages—which come by gesture, by facial expression, by allegory or symbol. Unfortunately, these messages are often missed or misinterpreted. We researched and wrote *Final Gifts* to help remedy that situation.

Our journey into Nearing Death Awareness began with a lunch-hour conversation with our coworkers. Such discussions often focused on the efforts of patients to communicate, and the difficulty of medical staffs in understanding confused messages. Everyone had a different story about some patient's attempts to get across a point; on one particular day, these stories suddenly seemed to come into focus—linked to one another by patterns of speech or gesture. Having listened to months of patients' seemingly incoherent comments, we decided to examine them, sensing that significant information was buried there. In analyzing these, we saw recurring themes hinting at significant patterns of communication. We undertook a study that eventually involved more than two hundred cases.

In each case, we looked for common factors that would explain the patterns. Did the patients using this language all have the same or similar disease processes—certain brain illnesses, bone diseases, and failure of the liver or kidneys—causing chemical imbalances that affected their perceptions? Had every patient's brain been deprived of oxygen for a time, altering his or her consciousness? Were imbalances in body fluids or body salts responsible for changes in behavior and mental clarity? Were all these patients on medications—for example, narcotics to control pain—that could cloud their thinking in similar ways? Any of these elements could bring about the kinds of "confused" communications displayed by our patients.

But we found no common cause for what we were seeing and hearing. Our patients had many different illnesses—varieties of cancer, different heart or lung diseases, birth defects, neurological ailments, AIDS. In some cases, their brain oxygen, body fluid, and body salt levels had been documented as normal. Their medications varied widely; some were taking no drugs at all, others many. In short, there was no apparent physiological explanation for their communication patterns.

Could culture, gender, age, or ethnicity have played a role? No. Our patients were males and females of all ages, and represented a variety of races, ethnic groups, and nationalities. They came from every type of religious background; some were agnostics or atheists.

But each had something to say, some message to convey. The

more data we collected and reviewed, the more excited we became as we began seeing that their messages fell into two main categories.

The first category of messages described what patients were experiencing: being in the presence of someone not alive, the need to prepare for travel or a change, mentions of some place they alone could see, their knowledge of when death would occur.

The second category consisted of messages about something, or someone, needed so death could be peaceful: the desire to reconcile personal, spiritual, or moral relationships, and requests to remove some barrier to achieving this peace.

As we learned more, we were able to interpret these messages for others and observe how this understanding helped not only patients but families and professional caregivers as well.

One of our biggest challenges was naming our theory. As patients got closer to death, they seemed to develop a special awareness of people, places, and things. This awareness evolved gently and gradually, as though they were drifting back and forth from a consciousness of this existence to an awareness of the next, intensifying as the patient was nearing death. The three key words were awareness, nearing, and death. Hence our choice of name: Nearing Death Awareness.

CHAPTER FOUR

REACTIONS TO DEATH

People react in many ways to the news of the impending death of someone they love. They may feel shock, disbelief, fear, anger, sadness—or, as often occurs, a continuously shifting blend of these and other strong emotions.

Immersed in these feelings, they wonder, "Does he know he's dying? Should I talk about it? What would I say?" They may ask themselves, "Should I tell her I'm sorry, or should I pretend that I don't know? Should I be bright and cheerful and try to lift her spirits? But it's terrible that she's dying, and I don't want her to think I don't care."

There's a reason for this awkwardness. Besides the absence of easy answers to questions like the ones above, death has become remote, no longer an integral part of life, but a fearsome and unwelcome visitor.

Once, the business of dying was a part of the business of living. With several generations of a family often residing under the same roof, children helped Mom and Dad care for Grandmother, who spent her last months on a bed in the living room. Or Grandfather came to live in what had been the sewing room; after his stroke, the doctor visited the house, examined the old man, and said, "There's no point in moving him—he'll be better off here in his own place with his own folks. Just keep him comfortable and call me if you need anything." In many coun-

tries, this remains the way people die: at home, cared for by
their families, with the process of dying a part of everyone's
life.

Today many families don't have close, frequent, or continuous
involvement with the one dying. Unlike earlier generations, they
don't learn how to be at ease with someone whose life is coming
to an end. Illness and death have been moved out of the house
and into the hospital or nursing home. Professionals provide the
care; relatives and friends become spectators watching something occur—not in a continuous stream of emotions and experiences from which to learn, but in awkward chunks of time,
determined by official visiting hours that leave them uncomfortable and unsatisfied.

Some health-care professionals don't want to spend any more
time or energy than necessary with dying patients. Many professionals believe in "protecting" patients and families from the
gravity of an illness, or the news of impending death. Operating
from that perspective, they may mislead families about a patient's chances for recovery by withholding or softening information. Others may limit family members' contact with the
person.

As spectators, people not only have to cope with the pain of
knowing that someone they love is dying, but must do so in a
state of uncertainty, not sure of what to do, how to do it, or
when. Many people see death acted out mainly on television or
in the movies, where it is overdramatized and designed to fit
conveniently into a time slot. In real life, death isn't always a
handy matter of minutes or hours, but a gradual process that
can last weeks, months, sometimes years. Instead of a last-gasp
sprint, death can be a marathon.

In new circumstances, most people feel uncomfortable until
they've grown accustomed to the situations and their roles in
them. If you've had no experience with death, it's unrealistic
to expect that you'll feel comfortable and competent around a
dying person.

The Physical Process

As families and friends deal with the dying of someone they love, they're full of memories of the person, once whole in mind and body. Uneasy with the changes they now see, and fearful of changes to come, they suffer, too.

People often assume that in every case a given disease—emphysema, AIDS, cancer—brings the same type of death. But each death depends on many factors—the person's age, the progression of the illness, the presence or history of other health problems, and the systems or organs failing most quickly.

The last months of life for a person with a terminal illness can have many possible scenarios. Most people experience several troublesome symptoms; some have many, others seem to have none. A few people may feel and look comparatively unchanged until weeks or days before dying; some have episodes of acute illness interspersed with periods of feeling well; others undergo gradual declines. Some people die while asleep or in comas; others are aware, even communicative, until their last breaths.

During the last months of living with a terminal illness, troublesome symptoms can arise at any time, and health-care professionals try to anticipate those most likely to affect an individual.

For the layperson, the thought of caring for someone dying, especially at home, can be frightening and overwhelming. But the best care possible is usually that given by family and friends.

Some people have dry or sore mouths; weight loss, fragile skin, and reduced mobility can lead to pressure sores. Some people experience nausea and vomiting; others have problems with constipation or diarrhea. Some become incontinent. Some people develop coughs, or have difficulty breathing.

Some people have problems with bruising or bleeding, or develop bones so brittle that they can snap when bumped. Some treatments cause hair loss, bloating and weight gain, or rashes.

Many people assume that terminal patients, especially those with cancer, will have pain. That's not always so; some have no pain, others have mild to moderate pain that can be controlled

with ease. A few people have pain so severe that expert assessment and care are needed to bring it under control.

Some patients are calm; others have periods of extreme anxiety, manifested by fidgeting or picking at the bedcovers. This
unsettled state may escalate until the person is extremely agitated. Some conditions cause dementia—the loss of the ability
to think, remember, or reason. Sometimes people seem to reverse
their schedules, sleeping most of the day, becoming more alert
at nightfall. This can exhaust caregivers.

The sense of taste can change—foods that were favorites
become bitter or unappealing. In a change that can be frustrating
for family and health-care workers in nonhospice settings, many
people lose interest in food and fluids—seemingly part of the
body's "slowing down."

A dying person's most common symptoms are weakness and
fatigue. Most people weaken to the point that they have difficulty
doing anything for themselves. They may become unable to
walk, to turn themselves in bed, to concentrate on a conversation, or even to open their eyes. They may spend much of the
day resting or sleeping. Often the sleep deepens, and the sleeper
slips into unconsciousness; gradually the breathing slows and
stops.

When Death Is Close

It's hard to predict the time of death, but there usually are
signs that death is likely to occur within hours or a few days.

One sign is difficulty swallowing. If the person has been
showing little appetite for food and water, the family may not
realize this inability is more than merely lack of interest. The
resulting dehydration usually isn't troublesome, and actually can
increase a dying person's comfort, by reducing the incidence of
some uncomfortable symptoms such as vomiting, pain, or difficulty in breathing. It's better not to put small amounts of fluids
into the mouth hoping the person will swallow; if she can't, the
fluid runs into the lungs. When a person no longer can swallow,
she doesn't need fluids; it's sufficient to cleanse the mouth with
moist sponges and to moisten the lips with a little cream. At

this juncture many medicines may be discontinued; others can be given in ways other than by mouth.

Sometimes mucus gathers in the mouth, throat, or lungs, and air flowing past it makes a rattling noise. This doesn't necessarily mean the person is having difficulty breathing. Turning the patient onto his side often reduces the rattling. If he does have difficulty breathing, oxygen may be used, or medicines to dry the mucus or to keep air passages open.

As death nears, a person's breathing may change—become irregular, speeding up for a while, then slowing down, even pausing for several seconds before starting again. Or the breathing may be louder for a while, then very faint and quiet.

The body's temperature may rise, while at the same time the hands and feet cool, perhaps turning blue or becoming mottled; sometimes the lips and nails turn blue. Generally neither the raised temperature nor the cool extremities and mottled skin disturb patients, and they require no treatment. Some people experience periods of profuse sweating, and need frequent sponging, dry linens, and good skin care. Output of urine and stool usually drops, with the urine becoming darker. Increased weakness may lead to incontinence.

A few people have involuntary movements, not unlike the twitches that happen when you're falling asleep. These don't usually bother the dying person; if they do, medicines can relieve them.

As the person gets weaker and sleepier, communication with others often becomes more subtle. Many people want the company of one or two important people. Often they pay little attention to what is going on; they seem not to listen, or their eyes become glazed—as if they're looking at, but not seeing, people or things. Sometimes their eyes remain half open, whether they're awake or asleep. But even when people are too weak to speak, or have lost consciousness, they can hear; hearing is the last sense to fade.

These changes can happen in the hours before death, two or three days before, or sometimes earlier. One or two signs may come weeks or months before. Experienced professionals know the signals indicating that death is truly imminent.

Provided any uncomfortable symptoms are well managed, death can be peaceful. The most obvious sign of death is an end to breathing. If breathing has been very quiet, or alternately slowing down and speeding up, you may have trouble deciding whether it actually has stopped. Sometimes the last few breaths sound like sighs. If the dying person is alert, you may see a slight smile or a look of farewell, or notice the eyes lose focus, then close. If he or she is asleep or unconscious, you may hardly realize what has happened.

When describing the dying people in this book, we haven't given much detail about their physical conditions. It's not that we want to minimize the effect of physical deterioration, but *Final Gifts* isn't about the physical care of the dying. It is about Nearing Death Awareness, and its message can help balance your sadness and exhaustion.

In spite of the body's breakdown, dying people who develop Nearing Death Awareness can find peace, comfort, and healing of emotional and spiritual pain. By anticipating, seeing, and learning from Nearing Death Awareness, families can be more aware of the part of the person they love that is much more than the physical self.

Physical changes do cause many emotional difficulties for the person dying, as well as for family and friends. When a father becomes incontinent and his son must clean and change him . . . when a husband no longer can brush his teeth and his wife must moisten his dry, sticky mouth . . . when a brother is in pain and his sister must give him medicine . . . these occasions can demonstrate great love. They also can generate great pain and lead to many feelings and questions more difficult to cope with than physical needs.

When someone you love is dying, you'll always be dealing with sadness. But your response to that sadness depends on many elements, often related to your previous experience with death.

If you haven't had much experience or haven't had role models who showed you how to behave around dying people, how can you manage? There is no "right" way to help a dying person, but the following pages contain some suggestions.

Understanding Your Feelings About Death

What is it like for those who are dying and for those who love them? What are your questions and anxieties? If you were dying, would you be angry that we can put people in space but haven't found a cure for your terminal illness? Would you resent having to give up your job to someone less qualified but healthier? Would you hate being dependent on others? Would you feel frustrated at having to relinquish control over so many aspects of your life? Would you be frightened of what dying might feel like? Would you be scared of what happens after death?

It isn't necessary that you have answers to all your questions; most people don't. But identifying your concerns, fears, and preferences can help avoid misunderstandings with a dying person, whose concerns, fears, and preferences may differ from yours.

For example, you might abhor the idea of being hospitalized and prefer to die at home. However, your dying friend might feel more secure in a hospital.

Or consider the question of when to discontinue treatment— often a very difficult decision arrived at by a dying person only after much thought, discussion, and emotional pain. Don't challenge such a decision, support it. You can do this more easily if you reflect on what you'd prefer, and see how your outlook parallels or diverges from the perspective of the one dying. It's important not to force your concept of dying onto someone else; let that person's ideas about death take precedence.

What the Dying Person Feels

After exploring your feelings, try to imagine those of the dying person. By trying on the idea of dying you'll have a surer sense of what to say and how to help. At this point it's worth reflecting on the stages of dying as described by Dr. Kübler-Ross: denial, anger, bargaining, depression, acceptance.

Although Dr. Kübler-Ross has labeled these experiences "stages," a person doesn't necessarily progress through them in orderly fashion. These emotions aren't exclusive to dying, either; any crisis or major life change can trigger them, which means that they will be familiar to almost any adult. These feelings often are easier to understand if we see them in the context of what dying people are trying to accomplish: they're struggling to accept the reality of their diagnosis, to adjust to life with illness, and to prepare for approaching death. These are enormous tasks; it's no surprise that the emotions accompanying them are varied and painful, sometimes difficult to understand, even overwhelming.

Denial

Denial is the refusal to accept reality, and grows out of shock. Told an illness is incurable and fatal, people often respond by saying, "I don't believe it! You must have made a mistake! This can't be true—I'm going to get a second opinion!" Sometimes they think, "Well, maybe most people with this illness die, but I'm going to beat the odds."

Denial can be expressed in behavior. Getting a second opinion on any grave diagnosis is a wise step, but seeking several "second" opinions may be a way of trying to avoid the truth. Denial also can take the form of refusing or "forgetting" to take medicines or keep appointments for treatment.

Why do people engage in denial? When we receive news too painful to absorb, we use denial to protect ourselves, to buy time during which we can adjust to a new and grim reality. Assuming a dying person understands his terminal diagnosis, respect expressions of denial. When you encounter them, don't challenge. It's not wise to try to make a dying person "face up to reality." Most people abandon the denial defense, usually as they become sicker or weaker, but many go back and forth between acceptance and denial. A person who yesterday was talking realistically about not getting any better may suddenly say, "When I get well, we can go camping again!"

It's harsh—as well as cruel and unnecessary—to try to break

down the denial with a response such as "You know you're much too sick; you're never going to get well, and you're never going camping again." However, neither should you reinforce or encourage a refusal to face reality by going along with it. Don't lie—it makes you a partner in denial, and though false cheer may seem momentarily comforting, eventually the person will move out of this stage and may want to talk with you about dying. If you've conveyed reluctance to face reality, the dying person will hesitate to talk with you about death, and may feel unsupported or even abandoned by you.

If you should neither challenge nor encourage denial, what should you do? You should recognize the wish or desire behind it. When your dying friend talks about getting better and going camping again, you could say, "Wouldn't that be fun!" or "I bet you'd like that!" These responses acknowledge your friend's hopes and wishes without reinforcing denial.

In some people, denial can be iron-clad and permanent.

AMELIA

As I arrived for my first visit with Amelia, eighty-seven, her son greeted me in the driveway.

'Please don't say anything to Mother about hospice or cancer," he said. "She often seems confused and doesn't know about her illness. It would only upset her if you mentioned it."

I introduced myself to Amelia as a nurse who would be stopping by to see how she was doing.

"Lovely!" she replied.

I asked about her medical history. She responded in great detail about her children's births some sixty years before, her gall-bladder surgery at forty-five and bunion removal ten years later, along with a variety of dental surgery. Not once did she mention having lost both breasts to mastectomies only three years ago, or the chemotherapy and radiation treatments she'd been undergoing since then. I excused myself and went down-

stairs to ask her son if the doctors had explained his mother's
illness, surgery, and treatments to her.

"Yes," he said with a smile. "Many times."

Back in Amelia's bedroom, I finished listening to her chest
with my stethoscope.

"What happened here?" I asked, pointing to the scars left by
the removal of her breasts. She looked down with great surprise.

"Well, for heaven's sake!" she said.

Amelia lived another year in comfort and happiness; I visited
twice a week, but she never "remembered" who I was or why
I'd come. She completed each day's *New York Times* crossword
puzzle with great accuracy, but never mentioned her illness,
and neither did I.

What if the denial comes not from the dying person but from
others? Friends and family often engage in denial longer than
a dying person. The news is too hard to bear; they pretend it
isn't there. Normal and understandable, this reaction nonethe-
less can be hard on a sick person. Family members may make
comments like "You look so much better today!" If true, this is
fine. But if untrue, what she hears is the other person's inability
or unwillingness to deal with the truth.

A person may try to break through the family's denial by
saying, "I know I'm very ill and that I won't get better." But
often the family's response leads him to decide the truth is too
painful. A strange conspiracy arises, in which everyone pretends
the patient will recover. It takes tremendous energy to sustain
this fiction—energy that is in short supply for the one who is
ill. The weight of another's denial adds to a patient's burden,
often causing a dying person to withdraw from those who are
denying, increasing his sense of isolation.

Anger

Dying people may feel angry. It's not unusual to hear someone
with a terminal illness ask, "Why is this happening?" Some
people feel angry at God for allowing them to get sick, at their

doctors for not being able to find a cure, at the government for putting money into weapons instead of medical research, or at the world in general. No matter how it's directed, most anger will be expressed to those who are closest and safest—family and friends. In the presence of such vehemence, it's very hard to avoid feeling hurt. Responding sharply often leads to arguments, which rarely accomplish anything. Besides not working, attempts to talk a person out of the anger—"Now, you know the doctors did everything they could . . . You should be grateful, things could be worse"—may intensify the patient's feelings. You could wind up being perceived as making light of the patient's concerns or taking the "enemy's" side.

It's more useful to look for the cause. Think of anger as a feeling that develops from another emotion. In people who are terminally ill, the roots of anger often are frustration, resentment, or fear.

Frustration can stem from helplessness at losing control and becoming dependent on others; resentment, from seeing others' lives go on; fear, from uncertainty about what dying is like.

DAN

Diagnosed with widespread incurable cancer at thirty-three, Dan was a very angry young man. Before his diagnosis he had done well at balancing the responsibilities of working as an electrician, being a husband and father, and leading his son's Cub Scout troop. Within ninety days, however, he was too weak to get out of bed or brush his teeth. He had to quit working. If he wanted a drink of water, medicine to relieve his rapidly increasing pain, or to use the toilet, he needed assistance. He couldn't help raise his children, or do even the most minor chores. His wife was always busy managing the household or finding others to assist her, and Dan's complaints about how her tossing and turning while asleep caused him pain had driven her to take a bed in an adjoining room.

When Dan was admitted to the hospice program, we guessed

that most of his anger grew out of frustration at his helplessness. He'd lost his livelihood. His roles as husband and father had shrunk. He had no control over his illness, and was forced to rely on others to satisfy even very basic needs.

All this made perfect sense—but logic isn't necessarily a salve to anger. Instead of trying to explain Dan's anger to him, we responded to the emotion that lay beneath it. Our goal wasn't to diminish his anger, but to decrease his feelings of helplessness by increasing his sense of being in control.

We began by letting Dan direct everything possible—meals, visitors, bathing arrangements. Small matters, true; but they were Dan's to control. We respected his wishes, letting him see that he had a degree of autonomy, as well as our empathy. This was the beginning of helping him understand and work through his anger.

Dan's bitter comments and snarled requests for assistance went from being constant to being intermittent. One morning as he finished a litany of complaints about how badly he'd slept, I said gently, "It sounds like you had a rough night."

"You're damn right it was rough," he snapped. Then he nodded and sighed. His eyes filled with tears, and he spoke again.

"You have no idea how bad it is at night," he said, looking at his wife. "I hate waking up in pain, and needing Elaine to get my pills. Sometimes she doesn't hear me, so I try to wait, but the pain gets worse. I hate not being able to manage the pills myself, and having to bother her. I wish she'd sleep in here, but I know she needs her rest."

Now it was Elaine's turn to be angry. "But you told me it made the pain worse when I turned over in bed," she said, with tears in her eyes. "There's just no pleasing you!"

"Dan, it sounds as if you're missing Elaine," I said. This unlocked a flood of emotions; Dan wept as he tried to explain to Elaine how sad and lonely he felt. She responded by explaining how it hurt her to sleep away from him, thinking he didn't want her around.

They made a deal; Elaine would return to their bed, with the pain pills and a glass of water beside her on the night table.

Dan could wake her without any effort; she could reach over, give him the pills, and hold the straw to his lips while he swallowed. Then they could return to sleep or lie awake together and talk. Dan lived only three more weeks, but they were better than many of the weeks that had gone before.

"Some of our best conversations were in the middle of the night," Elaine said later. "He often said he slept better with me there, and I know it was better for me. Sometimes we'd talk about the early years of our marriage, and his hopes for the boys, and how awful it was that he'd gotten sick. We'd cry because we didn't know how we'd manage without one another. It sounds sad, and it was, but it was a lot better than yelling at each other, as we'd been doing. That last week, I'd wake up some nights and he'd be lying there watching me. He'd smile and I'd put my arms around him and we'd go right back to sleep."

Dan and Elaine were able to break down the wall of anger they'd built to separate themselves from one another, and in doing so were able to talk about the emotions that had made them angry at one another, at themselves, at the whole situation. It wasn't easy to tear down that wall, but it brought them closer at a time when they needed to be as close as possible.

If you're encountering anger in a sick friend or relative, and suspect that helplessness is behind it, try to empathize. Say something like "I imagine it's hard to have to ask for help all the time" or "This seems as if it's very frustrating for you." Whenever possible, give the dying person choices and control. Respond to the frustration, not the anger.

Anger also can result from resentment, perhaps at seeing coworkers, friends, or family members enjoy responsibilities, opportunities, and futures denied the one dying.

L I Z

Liz, a nurse, was dying of breast cancer at thirty-two. When diagnosed she was working in a small hospital in her hometown. After receiving treatment several hundred miles away, she returned to spend her last months in the hospital where she'd worked.

These were difficult months for everyone involved. Besides disfigurement, Liz was experiencing a great deal of physical pain. Her former coworkers were saddened by her situation, but also irritated by the steady stream of complaints from an often angry Liz.

The nurses on the unit where Liz was dying noticed a pattern. Several times a week, former coworkers would bring lunch to Liz's room. They'd talk about what was happening on her old unit, about how patients Liz had known were doing, and about new cases and treatments. During lunch, Liz would get grumpier and grumpier; all afternoon, and into the evening, she'd be snappy and hostile.

One night a nurse who often took care of Liz on the evening shift brought up the subject.

"You seem upset," she said. "Is it something I can help you with?"

"No, I'm just in a bad mood," Liz replied. "I always seem to be in a bad mood."

"Always?"

"Well, no," Liz said after a moment's reflection. "A lot of times in the evening I find I have no patience. Everyone seems to get on my nerves. You must have noticed."

"Yes, I did," the nurse said, sitting in the chair beside Liz's bed. "I've also noticed that it seems to happen on particular days."

"What do you mean?" Liz asked.

"Well, I come in at three in the afternoon. Whenever the day nurse tells me one of the staff from your old wing has been by for lunch, I know I'll find you upset."

Liz thought about that and nodded.

"That's true," she said. "It's worse on days when they've been here. They really bug me."

The nurse asked how the visits usually went; Liz described their conversations and said that at one time she'd enjoyed them.

"I liked catching up on all the patients and the gossip," she said. "It was fun, and it made me feel I was back home again. But it doesn't feel like that anymore."

"What does it feel like now?" the nurse asked.

Liz was quiet for a minute or two. "I know this will sound childish and awful, but they make me mad when they come in here and tell me what's happening on *my* unit," she said. "Sooner or later, they go back to work, and take over what I want to be doing. I have to lie here in this stupid hospital and die!"

Liz's anger arose from resentment at her former colleagues' good health, vitality, and open-ended futures. Seeing what was happening, those caring for Liz were able to alter the pattern that fueled her anger. With Liz's permission, the evening nurse spoke to some of her former coworkers, who had frustrations of their own.

"Liz didn't use to be like this," one said. "It's very hard to spend any time with her; I guess I'll come back and see her when she's through being angry."

The evening nurse explained what she thought was happening, and suggested possible approaches. The next day a friend from the old nursing unit began a lunch visit in Liz's room with a different comment.

"I bet you get tired of us talking shop all the time," she said. "What would you like to talk about?"

Liz mentioned her love of gospel music, and they spent an enjoyable half hour singing along with one of her favorite tapes.

Another former coworker, quite comfortable with expressing her feelings, visited later that week. She directly addressed the fact of Liz's illness.

"I miss you a lot at work," she said. "I feel so sad about what's happening to you."

This led to a heartfelt discussion of their friendship, their mutual sadness, and their expectation that they would meet in another world. Full of hugs and tears, that visit ended on a note of special closeness for both women.

Anger may grow out of fear. Most people have at least some fear of dying. When dying people talk about their fears, many of them say, "I'm not afraid to be dead; it's what happens before I die that bothers me." Gentle exploration of such statements often leads to clearer expression of fears: "I'm afraid of what dying may be like. Will it hurt? What's it like?"

Many people are also scared to discuss their fears of death. Late one evening—such fears often surface in the middle of the night—Helen said, "What's dying like?" but before I could respond added, "No, don't tell me." She feared the answer might make it worse, but my simple explanation relieved her anxieties, because what she had imagined was much worse than reality.

Some people can say clearly, "I'm afraid it will hurt, I don't think I can take a lot of pain." Others may say, "I've always believed in God; faith has always been a very important part of my life, but now I find myself wondering if it's all true, whether God really will be there after I die. What if there's nothing after all?"

If a person can't put his fears into words, or says, "I'm scared of the whole thing!" it may be useful to ask about his experiences with death or find out what his questions are. Different experiences breed different fears and needs. Some people are simply afraid of the symptoms of their illnesses. Knowledge of a person's history and outlook can aid in exploring these fears. Once understood, they can be discussed with the appropriate person. A doctor or nurse can answer such questions as "What will my physical death be like?" or "Will I suffer?" A priest, minister, or rabbi may be the person with whom to discuss fears related to God. Some patients' anger grows out of fear that sustenance or medical treatment is prolonging their discomfort, rather than improving the quality of their lives.

GORDON

Dying made Gordon very angry. Sullen in the company of family and friends, he was belligerent with his doctors and nurses, frequently cursing them—not at all the way he'd been when he was well.

We looked for patterns. There really was no time when Gordon wasn't angry, but when did his ire worsen? When did it ease? What precipitated an outburst?

Gordon was angriest with his doctors and nurses, especially when they were giving him his medicines. One day, talking with his priest, Gordon said he didn't trust medical people; he feared they'd find another treatment and persuade him to try it, rather than letting him die in peace.

"All these people do is prolong my suffering," he said.

It helped a bit when his doctor said there wouldn't be any more treatments, but what really helped was a different approach. When nurses brought Gordon his medicines, they would take care to say gently, "These are to keep you comfortable. They're not to prolong your dying." Gordon still glared, and never grew warm and friendly, but gradually he became less agitated, the source of his anger quenched.

Anger related to terminal illness has numerous possible sources. Many emotions arise out of the losses people experience as they face dying. Identifying these emotions isn't always easy, but trying to understand them makes it easier to respond helpfully to the anger.

Bargaining

The easiest way to understand the bargaining aspect of dying is to watch a child at bedtime. One more hug, one more story, one more drink of water—how inventive they can be as they try to stay up a few minutes longer!

Dying people do the same thing as they try to postpone the inevitable. They bargain with God. If they don't believe in God, they bargain with anyone they think might have the power to extend life a little longer.

Many bargains revolve around treatments. "I'll take this chemotherapy," people say to themselves. "I'll stick to a healthy diet. I won't complain, so God will let me live until my grand-child graduates."

People with AIDS often make deals to spend the time they have left working to stop the epidemic. "I'll get involved," they may think. "I'll take care of others. I'll teach people how not to get infected. But, God, if I do this you have to let me live longer." Amazingly, such bargains often seem to work.

Most dying persons' deals go unnoticed; the bargains usually remain secret. If a dying person does bring up the subject, listen with respect and say something like "Wouldn't that be great!" or "We'll help in any way we can."

Depression

A dying person's depression grows out of grief. Dying people grieve as anyone does for something that is lost. But their grief has two parts; they're mourning what's lost already to illness— health, family role, job, independence—but also for what will be lost when they die—personal relationships, life itself, and the future.

Most of us have plans and dreams: children we'll have, trips we'll take, books we'll write, new careers we'll start. Acknowl-edging the reality of death's approach means abandoning these possibilities. Because they're lost, they must be mourned.

These feelings of sadness and depression should be honored, not dismissed or diluted. To dying people, comments along the lines of "Look on the bright side" or "You've had a good life" or "We've all got to die sometime" seem like attempts to minimize or make light of their emotional pain. All you can do when they voice these feelings is listen. Often, no answer is needed—only the attempt to understand.

MARK

Mark's cancer, which everyone had thought was cured, returned so extensively that he had little time to live. He sounded very sad, talking at length about how much it hurt to know he'd be leaving his wife, Joyce, and his young children. It was no consolation that he and Joyce had done all they could to prepare the kids for a future without Daddy. Mark knew how strong Joyce was, and that she had friends to call on for support after he was gone.

He didn't need cheering up. He didn't need someone to say, "I'll help raise your children" or "I'll try to be there for Joyce after you're gone." He didn't need anyone to say, "Well, at least your cancer isn't painful, at least you've had time to prepare for this, at least you've done something worthwhile with your life."

What Mark needed was to have someone listen to his pain, empathize with his sadness, and share his tears.

Acceptance

Acceptance is a feeling of peaceful resignation that usually doesn't come to stay until death is very close. It's common for patients to experience interludes of acceptance and then, in one day, in one conversation, in one sentence, slip into another emotional stage. But eventually death nears, at which time permanent acceptance may arrive. When this occurs—provided a dying person is comfortable—she needs little except the presence of one or two important people.

If you are one of these people, you may experience mixed emotions. The peace of another's acceptance of death can be comforting, but with acceptance comes detachment, a drawing away from others no matter how close they have been. This can be painful for those being left behind.

MAX

A year before Max was to retire, he and his wife, Paula, began to plan a cross-country trip. During his last week on the job, Max was diagnosed as having cancer. His retirement began not with a transcontinental journey but with eighteen months of treatments, prescriptions, hospital stays, increasing weakness, and fewer periods of feeling well. Throughout this period, Max raged at life's unfairness, and swore he'd get better.

"I don't want to be sick. I want to be looking at the Grand Canyon!" he told Paula. "I don't want to die! I don't want to leave you! I want us to have the fun we'd planned!"

But Max never made the trip, and in his last days of life he lay in bed, barely speaking, his communication limited to a loving smile each time Paula rubbed his back or brought his medicine or spooned him a taste of ice cream. He seemed completely comfortable and completely at peace—in contrast to Paula, who was neither.

"I know I should be glad he's not suffering, that he's not in pain, that he's not fighting anymore," she said. "But I'm not glad! I don't want him to be like this—it feels so awful! It makes me feel so selfish to say it, but he seems to be happy that he's leaving me! It's like he's going and he's happy to be going and I can't stand it!"

Max was letting go—of the trip they'd planned, of his desire for a cure, even of his regret at leaving his wife. He was able to let go because he'd worked through his grief and was ready to die. To Paula this felt like rejection; Max was pulling away from her, it was painful, and yet she felt embarrassed to be taking it that way.

This is not an uncommon reaction. Many people think they should be concerned only with the dying patient's needs, with the end of that person's suffering. But we also are concerned with ourselves and our own losses. Paula wanted Max to stop fighting and die in peace, but she didn't want him to leave her, and it hurt. The most important way to help her was to let her cry, to listen to her grief without judging, and to empathize with her pain.

Most dying people—as well as their families and friends—
go back and forth among the stages of dying, shifting from
anger to denial to acceptance to bargaining to depression—many
times, in no apparent order, and not necessarily in synchroni-
zation.

JULIA

As Julia was finishing six weeks of radiation for extensive and
inoperable lung cancer, her family could see she wasn't getting
better, and in fact seemed to be getting worse. She and her
husband talked with the doctor, who confirmed everyone's
fears—she had perhaps three months to live. They told their
two adult daughters, who lived in the neighborhood, and their
son, John, who lived on the West Coast.

When I arrived the next afternoon Julia's daughter Jane, a
former nurse who was providing much of her mother's care,
was weeping in the kitchen.

"It's so hard to cope with this," she said. "Last night my
mother was saying doctors never know anything, and that she'll
be fine if she can only start eating again. That made Dad really
mad; he yelled at her and then stormed out of the house. He
didn't come back for hours, and when he did he'd been drinking.
This morning my sister Sally calls to talk about getting in touch
with a funeral home, and she can't figure out why I can't stop
crying. Then my brother calls from California to tell me about
some new chemotherapy; he wants to know if Mom's doctor
knows about it. Is this family going crazy, or is it just me?"

We started by talking about her sadness and pain. Her mother's prognosis was no surprise; in her hospital work Jane had
cared for many cancer patients.

"I knew she was deteriorating, so I thought I was ready for
this," she said. "I didn't think it would be so hard."

This occurs frequently. Health-care professionals often assume that because they understand what's happening to someone they love the pain somehow will be eased. But knowledge
only provides understanding; it doesn't diminish pain.

Jane realized she was grieving and depressed, but was grateful that she at least was dealing with reality. She went over the reactions of others in the family.

"Mother's in denial, but that won't last long," she said. "She's known for a while that she's getting worse; last week she even told me she doesn't want to go on like this. Dad, of course, will be hopeless. He's always hiding his feelings behind angry words and drink."

Then she laughed and pointed to the heap of sodden tissues on the kitchen counter.

"But this generation isn't doing too well, either," Jane said. "John's a real wheeler-dealer. I bet he thinks he can find Mom a deal that'll fix everything. And Sally—she'll be calm, controlled, and accepting for a while, then fall apart when something changes."

When I visited a couple of days later Jane had an update.

"We all changed roles," she said. "I yelled at Dad for drinking. He and Mom had a long talk about funeral plans; Mom had him call the priest. Father Wheeler came over and they put together a ceremony, and Dad's been crying all evening.

"Now Mom's working on a list of what she wants the grandchildren to have," Jane continued. "She collects music boxes, and she's tagging her favorites so we know who gets which one. Sally telephoned the doctor to see if that new drug might work, and John called to say he hadn't slept the last few nights, worrying that he might not see Mom before she died. So he's coming home this weekend."

In short order, Jane had gone from depression to anger, Mom from denial to acceptance, Dad from anger to depression, Sally from acceptance to bargaining, and John from bargaining to depression, then acceptance. And these were only the emotions Jane reported or observed. This is a very simplistic example of what happens to family emotions when someone is dying— everyone in Jane's family probably ran the gamut, and it's possible to experience several emotions at the same time.

Each person involved has a set of feelings; each brings to the situation a history of experiences and a pattern of behaviors.

To some degree, most people die—and react to someone else's death—in ways reflecting their usual style of handling of crises. Quiet people remain quiet; angry, controlling people continue to be angry and controlling; people known for taking care of others may be trying to do so with their last breaths.

Struggling for the Proper Response

How do you respond to these feelings? What if the patient is in denial, the spouse is angry, the daughter depressed, the son bargaining, the best friend accepting? The first step may be the hardest: Keep still. Don't try to help anyone "deal with" denial, anger, and depression in order to achieve acceptance, which many people see as the "correct" response to dying. Acceptance can be more comfortable than the other stages—especially for onlookers—but there is nothing right or wrong or well or poorly adjusted about any of the stages of dying. They're normal, predictable responses to a process.

Try not to give advice or to look for solutions. Listen. Accept. This is difficult; if you really listen, you will hear pain, even feel it. If only to relieve your own distress, you'll be tempted to offer advice or to attempt to defuse the anger—to say *something* to avoid the pain and sadness. Unfortunately, there is really no way of doing so.

Feeling Useful

How deeply will you be involved? If your spouse, child, or parent is the one dying, you may be responsible for most or much of the care, and so will be around most of the time. If the dying person is a friend, you need to think about how much you can be involved. The amount of time you spend with an acquaintance who is ill probably will differ from that spent with one to whom you're very close. The degree of involvement that seems to work best is the same or a little more than before illness set in, but it's important to decide consciously how great or little that involvement will be.

If you decide not to visit or to be involved in a friend's dying, you may find it helpful to do something to recognize what is taking place. Many people find that sending flowers, cards, or a brief note saying, "I'm thinking of you," allows them to feel they've acknowledged the situation. If you avoid thinking about how much or little to see the person, or if you think about it but avoid making a decision, feelings of guilt may cause you stress before and after the death.

"I let her down," you may say to yourself. "I should have called. Now I'm sorry I didn't do more."

Many dying people are lonely, not only because people don't visit, but also because of what happens when people *do* visit. Visitors may spend their time with the person wrapped up in idle talk about the weather, sports, or politics. Perhaps because, consciously or unconsciously, it's intended to do so, their chatter keeps the dying person from being able to speak intimately. A dying person's world shrinks, narrowing to a few important relationships and the progress of his illness. When dying people aren't allowed to talk about what's happening to them, they become lonely, even amid loving, concerned people. They may feel isolated and abandoned, and in turn become resentful and angry.

This is why it's important to reflect in advance about how to help and what to say.

JEAN

Not long before her death, Jean wrote, "When the friend who was my main caregiver had to be away for a few days, people told her if I needed anything I was to call them. Several told me so personally. But only one person made a specific offer.

" 'I know you go to church when you're able to,' she said. 'I'd like to take you on Sunday. I'll be over for you at ten. Don't worry if you decide at the last minute that you can't make it. It won't inconvenience me at all.'

"That call was a real relief," Jean wrote. "I can't take everyone up on casual offers that require me to ask for help, but I really

appreciate it when someone suggests something they can do—
and does it!"

If you want to help with practical chores, offer specifically
rather than generally. Don't say, "Call me if I can do anything"
or "Let me know if I can help." Not only are dying people too
overwhelmed to make lists of tasks for someone else to do, they
may not know what needs doing, or may wonder if you're simply
being polite. Instead, offer something concrete.

"I know you enjoy music," you could tell a friend. "May I
bring over some CDs or tapes tomorrow?"

Offer to do the grocery shopping. Propose to vacuum or dust
the house. Always give the sick person the option of canceling
at the last minute. And by adding, "If that's not what you want,
tell me what else I can do," you ease the way for the person to
make a request.

If you're the main caregiver, be willing to accept help—the
assistance and involvement of others will ease your sense of
being overburdened. However, when someone makes a generic
offer to help, be ready to say, "Thanks—here's what I need you
to do. . . ." Friends often want to do something but don't know
what; they'll feel better if you can give them specific assign-
ments, and you'll have more energy for other things.

Talking About Death

Talk of death is among the most difficult of issues. You may
worry that you'll say something that will "make it worse."

People often think that if they mention death they'll upset
someone who is ill. Many worry that if they try to say anything
about something as sad as a friend's dying they may break into
tears and cause the dying person to do so as well. The control
that goes into maintaining such composure is sometimes perceived as a display of indifference.

SONIA

Sonia complained about her children's efforts to be very brave and calm.

"They should cry!" she said. "After all I did for them, they should be sorry I'm dying!"

Her son was taken aback.

"But, Ma, we didn't want to make it worse for you," he said. "You know you've never been able to stand seeing one of us upset; you always cried with us."

"I thought it was because you didn't care!" she said.

Remember that not saying anything gives the appearance of not caring. Many factors figure in the depth and intimacy with which you and the patient discuss death and dying. If the person is trying to believe the diagnosis, learning to live with the illness, and preparing for death, you may conclude that it would be helpful to approach the subject, and often it is.

However, the person may not be ready or have the energy to talk about death. Perhaps she has someone else to talk with, wants to spare you, or simply doesn't want to talk about it. Don't force the topic onto anyone, but don't shy away from it, either.

One way to begin talking about death is to let the dying person know of your interest. If you don't know whether the person will recover, asking, "Are you going to be all right?" or "Can you tell me what's happening?" may help you both get started. The first conversation usually is the most difficult; once you've broken the ice it becomes a little easier.

Show that you're willing to talk, then let the conversation develop. You might begin with a simple comment: "I'm sorry to hear that you're so ill," or "I really feel sad when I think about what's happening to you." Wait for a response. Listen. There is no one right thing to say, although it's never wrong to speak of your love and concern.

Don't worry about saying or doing the "wrong" thing. Most of us have said a few wrong things, and good relationships haven't suffered. Sick people usually tolerate mistakes made in honest, loving attempts to help.

What's often harder to forgive—whether for the dying person or in one's self—is the failure to do or say anything. Dying people need the company of those who will listen, those willing to understand their situations, those who continue to offer love and friendship in the face of death.

II

NEARING DEATH AWARENESS: WHAT I AM EXPERIENCING

.

THE following five chapters describe the experiences of dying people as they approach death. They may tell us they know they're dying, often by making reference to travel or change. Some tell of talking with, or sensing the presence of, people whom we cannot see, but who are with them as they move along their journeys. Some refer to the peace and beauty of another place invisible to those around them. Still others know—and even tell us—when they will die.

When dying people begin to have these experiences, they often seem preoccupied, distracted, perhaps even a little puzzled. They may ask questions, seem glassy-eyed, or appear to be looking through us, as if focused on something beyond. To draw another parallel with birthing, they look the way women in labor look—busy, working hard, and concentrating on what's happening to them.

Dying people are not bothered by these experiences, but find them generally pleasant, reassuring, even comforting. However, family members and friends may be upset by the patient's attempts to describe the experiences or fearful, believing the patient to be hallucinating, confused, or demented. Those who understand these descriptions for what they are—information about what it is like to be dying—can learn from the dying person, and share in the peace and comfort the dying derive from these experiences.

CHAPTER FIVE

"WHERE'S THE MAP?"

ELLEN

Ellen looked like a typical seventeen-year-old cheerleader—a blue-eyed blonde, pretty, bright, and full of personality. She'd excelled at all she'd done. A good student, she looked forward to attending college with her friends in the fall. But in September of her senior year, she developed a sharp pain in her right thigh.

At first she assumed she'd strained a muscle leading cheers for the football team. But the pain persisted and increased, and her leg became weak, so she saw a doctor. To her family's horror, X-rays showed cancer that had spread from somewhere else in her body to the bone of her leg.

Despite extensive testing, the original site of Ellen's cancer was never determined. The cancer already had spread to other bones—her ribs, left hip, and shoulder—eliminating amputation as an option. Radiation therapy was started immediately.

Ellen and her family reacted to this terrible news with silent numbness, but pulled closer to each other for support. She chose to view her cancer as a challenge rather than a catastrophe. Ellen's determination sparked the same reaction in her family and friends. Everyone pitched in to help her continue in school while taking her treatments.

Many times Ellen's brothers, teachers, and friends carried her books or pushed her wheelchair through the school corridors. A tutor worked with her at home when she was too weak to attend school. Somehow she maintained her grades and graduated with her class—to a standing ovation.

As her friends left for college that fall, she tearfully told them, "I'll see you next semester when I'm finished with my treatments!"

"We're a close Christian family," her mother said. "When one of us has a problem, we all share it. We fight our battles together." And fight they did.

"My princess is a fighter; cancer won't stop her!" her father said.

But cancer did stop her; the response to various treatments was poor, and her disease spread at an alarming rate. Ellen's dreams of college and growing up began to fade. Her interest in the larger world diminished; friends' visits no longer held her attention. She only wanted to be comfortable at home with her family.

Since nothing was helping, Ellen decided to stop the treatments; her "good times" were getting shorter and less frequent. As she got weaker and less able to care for herself, the doctor urged the family to call hospice for help and direction with the last stages of her illness. The family resisted.

"We don't need outsiders," the mother said. "We can manage by ourselves."

The doctor persisted. "Ellen's getting too weak to come to my office," he explained. "I don't make house calls and I want her to be monitored by professionals, so I can be sure she's as comfortable as possible."

"We trust your judgment, so we'll think about it," Ellen's father said. "We're afraid she'll think that everybody's given up on her if she hears the word 'hospice.' "

It was nearly a month before Ellen's parents called us; by then she'd deteriorated dramatically. She was now confined to bed and experiencing increasing pain.

When I drove into their driveway for my first visit, Ellen's father was standing resolutely in the yard waiting for me.

"You're not going to talk to her about dying, are you?" he asked. "We have to be strong for her."

I assured him that I was interested in getting to know Ellen and her family, and would only talk about things that she wanted to discuss. But, I said, I would question her a lot about her comfort. I particularly wanted Ellen to be at ease with me.

It's common, initially, for the family to greet the hospice nurse with a warning: "Don't say anything to her about dying. She doesn't know and she couldn't handle it!" Moments later, the patient tells the nurse privately: "Don't say anything to my family about my dying. They don't know and they couldn't handle it!" With support and encouragement both patient and family can end this compassionate conspiracy and move on to honest, open communication.

"She refuses to take any of her pain medication," Ellen's father said, leaning against my car. "She knows it's a narcotic and she doesn't want to become a drug addict."

"I'll work with Ellen's needs, in whatever manner she wants," I said. "It's important that she have the right information so she can do this her own way and as comfortably as possible."

Her father seemed relieved. "We just can't believe this is happening to her," he said, fighting back tears. "We really don't mean to make your job difficult, but she's suffered so much already, we don't want you to say or do anything that will upset her."

"I understand your concern," I said. "I think you'll all feel more comfortable when you know me a little better. How about if we just visit together for a little while?" I asked. Still somewhat wary, Ellen's parents allowed me in to meet their daughter.

Ellen's every bone was clearly defined by her severe weight loss, making her look like a fragile young colt. She was surrounded by big, fluffy pillows. Her mother and I sat on either side of the bed while her dad stood guard—positioning himself behind the head of her bed, where he could quickly signal me to stop, if the conversation was broaching a taboo subject.

Ellen seemed at ease and pleased to meet me. "It'd be great if you could give us some suggestions for making this easier on my folks," she said. "It's a lot of work for them."

"You know what, Ellen," I said, "that's just exactly what your parents said about you. I hear you've worked pretty hard yourself. So how about if we all work together to make this easier for everyone?" I asked. Ellen smiled in agreement and her father visibly relaxed.

The discussion gradually came around to pain and her fear of addiction.

"Would you take this medication if you weren't sick and in pain?" I asked. "Would you use this medication to escape from reality or because you liked feeling high?"

"Of course not!" Ellen replied indignantly.

I explained that fear of addiction is common. Some people become addicted by misusing pain medicines and tranquilizers. However, addiction is the result of using medications for physical *and* psychological needs. When medication is used properly for physical needs, addiction is usually not a problem. Physical tolerance can occur with a medication used over time, but is easily handled by increasing the dose to maintain comfort. I told her addiction must include psychological dependency, as well— it can't exist without *both* components. So, used in the proper context, pain medication need not cause addiction.

I explained that if Ellen took a smaller dose of her pain medication on a regular basis—even when she wasn't uncomfortable—she probably wouldn't have episodes of severe pain requiring the larger doses she'd been taking irregularly—nor would she be as sedated.

"I'll try it that way for two days and we'll see, okay?" she asked.

"Fine," I said. "We'll take it one step at a time. You're the boss!"

Afterward, Ellen's father walked me to my car.

"Does my visiting two or three times a week sound agreeable to you?" I asked. "I do think there's more that can be done to help you. Obviously, Ellen's as concerned about you and your wife as you are about her."

"Could we try it for a month and then decide?" he asked. It was clear that being in control was important to this family.

"Absolutely!" I said. "You can fire me anytime you want."

For almost a month the family did well caring for Ellen, and shared a quiet and tender time, until, one day, I received a frantic phone call from Ellen's mother.

"Get out here fast," she said. I could hear Ellen wailing in the background. "We're losing it!"

When I arrived, Ellen was thrashing around in bed, seeming anguished while her parents were trying in vain to soothe her.

"Where is the map?" she cried. "I'm lost!"

That morning, Ellen's parents had moved her downstairs to the room next to theirs. Her voice was becoming weaker and they feared they wouldn't hear her if she called for help during the night.

Thinking the move had confused her, they ran up and down the stairs bringing familiar items from her old room, in an attempt to reorient her. The more they ran and the more they brought down, the more confused and upset Ellen became. She pushed them away, her anxiety and frustration increasing.

"Where's the map?" she cried. "If I could find the map, I could go home! Where's the map? I want to go home!"

Her father had even rushed out and bought a map of her town and put it on the wall next to her bed, thinking that would help. But she only became more upset.

When the additional pain medication I gave didn't help, I took Ellen's parents aside.

"Could she be talking about another home?" I asked.

"We have no other home," her mother said. "But we've always referred to Heaven as our future home. Is that what she means? Do you think she's dying soon?"

"Ellen doesn't look as if she's dying soon," I said. "But as sick as she is it is certainly possible."

Her parents decided she might be referring to Heaven, and trying to tell them through her "confusion" that she'd be dying soon.

We went into Ellen's room. Her parents sat on either side of her bed, held her hands, and kissed her.

"Ellen, it's all right," they said. "You *will* find the map, and you *will* find your way; we understand what's happening, and we are here with you."

Ellen settled right down, became very peaceful, and drifted off to sleep. As her parents sat there stroking her hands, they too became peaceful. The crisis seemed resolved, so I quietly left.

The next day being Saturday, I asked the on-call nurse to check in on them.

"I called to tell them I'd be in the neighborhood," the nurse reported later. "Even though they said everything was okay, I said I'd like to just pop in for a quick visit sometime that afternoon.

"When I did, Ellen was rousable but very sleepy, and looked quite comfortable," she continued. "Her parents and brothers seemed fine—they were taking turns sitting with her and holding her hand. They had taken shifts through the night, so all of them could get some rest. I didn't see any problems.

"Ellen was sleeping, so they were all in the living room talking to me when she died without any warning at all—quietly and peacefully. We were so surprised, but Ellen's mother said, 'She worried so about this being too hard for all of us. Isn't it curious that she died when the nurse was here to be with us?' They gathered around her bed and held her, murmuring their good-byes. Crying, her mother said, 'She's home now. She found the map.' "

The dying often use the metaphor of travel to alert those around them that it is time for them to die. They also have a deep concern about the welfare of those they love, asking themselves, "Do they understand? Are they ready? Are they going to be all right?" It seems dying people need permission to die. If given, that permission provides great relief; its absence can make the dying process more difficult and lengthy. The dying intuitively know when—and often why—this permission is being withheld, by the behavior of those around them. This withholding indicates that those they love don't understand their struggle, nor are they prepared emotionally to deal with the finality of their leaving.

Look at the anguish of Ellen's parents—dashing up and down the stairs, bringing more items from Ellen's room—and look at Ellen's anxiety—wailing and thrashing around in bed, attempting unsuccessfully to communicate with her family. Compare these with the scene of Ellen resting peacefully, her family quietly holding her hands and being with her.

You can see how Ellen's family provided what she needed by letting her know they understood the messages she was so desperately trying to give them—"I am dying, it is time for my journey from this life, I need to know you understand and are ready; I need your permission to go."

If a family can understand and respond to a dying person as Ellen's family did, all involved can share the resulting comfort and peace.

CHAPTER SIX

PREPARING FOR TRAVEL OR CHANGE: "I'M GETTING READY TO LEAVE."

Contrary to popular belief, or perhaps from wishful thinking—because of our own discomfort with death—dying people know they are dying, even if no one else knows or has told them. They attempt to share this information by using symbolic language to indicate preparation for a journey or change soon to happen. Travel is a clear metaphor often used to describe this need to go forth—to die.

Many accept this knowledge of their impending death without anxiety or fear, but may need validation or information about what the dying will be like. Some experience apprehension, often due to deep concern that family and friends don't accept this reality or may be unprepared for the finality of their leaving.

DICK

At fifty-five, Dick was a quiet, affectionate man who'd spent his working years as a postman. He and his wife, Ruth, had raised four children in a rambling three-bedroom house that he'd expanded and kept up, using his considerable skills as a handyman. Never poor, they weren't wealthy, but times were getting better. The three older children had finished college and had good jobs; the youngest was about to graduate. For the first time, Dick and Ruth were saving money.

One of their dreams was to purchase a sailboat. After careful planning, they bought a twenty-foot craft that they named *Our Turn*. Every weekend, Dick and Ruth drove to the shore and spent hours there, often fixing dinner in the tiny galley and spending Saturday night aboard. In bad weather, they kept the boat in the slip, and busied themselves varnishing the woodwork and polishing the chrome while they talked of trips they would make when the skies cleared and the seas calmed.

But the better times lasted only two years. At fifty-seven Dick was diagnosed with pancreatic cancer, which had spread to his liver and both lungs. He and Ruth realized his was a terminal illness, but hoped treatment would buy him a little time.

It didn't buy him much. The side effects of chemotherapy were severe; it didn't seem to be delaying the cancer's growth, so his doctor recommended it be stopped. Dick was deteriorating rapidly. He was referred to a hospice program and admitted to the inpatient unit.

Ruth visited daily, going home each night to sleep. One evening, just after midnight, I checked to see if Dick needed anything.

"Well, how is the tide tonight?" Dick asked, taking me by surprise.

"I don't know," I said. "Would you like me to find out?"

Dick smiled. "Oh, no, it doesn't really matter," he said. "I won't be here when you come around again, anyway."

I asked Dick what he meant; he only smiled and looked off into space. I asked if he was trying to tell me something—that he might be changing in some way. The only response was a gentle smile. I saw no signs that death was near, but believed what he had said might be important. Telephoning Ruth, I described our conversation, and offered my interpretation—Dick might be letting us know he was changing, and might be about to die. Ruth said she'd have their son Scott drive her back to the hospice unit.

Returning to Dick's room, I told him I still didn't know about the tide, but that Ruth and Scott would be there in about an hour. Again he smiled.

I stayed with him until they arrived. During that interlude, he nodded or smiled in response to my questions and comments, but said little. When his wife and son entered the room, he smiled at them and closed his eyes for the last time.

He slept the rest of the night with Ruth beside him and Scott in the next room. Just before 5 A.M. his breathing stopped and he died.

As we waited for the funeral director to arrive, Ruth and Scott told me how glad they were to have been there when Dick died; I gave all the credit to Dick and his brief, simple message.

"But somehow it was just like him!" Ruth said. "He'd want to know about the tide, he'd want us to have a little warning, and he'd want me to be with him."

For their own particular reasons, some families are unable to understand and respond to such messages. It's important not to be critical, but rather to be sensitive to their needs as well. The dying person still has needs, but in such situations the responsibility falls to someone else—perhaps the nurse, the minister, or a friend.

GEORGE

Charming, articulate, and well organized—thanks in no small part to a career in the Army, from which he'd retired as a lieutenant colonel—George was in his mid-sixties. After the service George had built a second career as a consultant.

His first wife had died when he was forty-four; they'd had no children. At sixty-two, George had remarried; his new wife, Joan, had been widowed twice. Only eighteen months after their wedding George was diagnosed with colon cancer. He had surgery and seemed to be recovering well, but the cancer showed up in his liver and was incurable. For six months he deteriorated, becoming so weak that he had to give up the reading he loved; after a headline or two, he'd drop the newspaper, too tired to go on.

We found him a volunteer, an ex-military man himself, who would visit and read to him. That was a relief for Joan, who took advantage of his help to go shopping with her daughter or spend time with her grandchildren.

One day when I arrived, she greeted me sadly.

"Well, he's out of it now," she said. "He doesn't make any sense at all."

I asked why she thought that.

"He keeps asking me to get his papers, his passport, and his ticket," Joan said, looking troubled and twisting a handkerchief around her fingers.

I mentioned that talk of travel often is a way that dying people talk of death; I asked if she thought that might be so with George.

"No, no," Joan said. "His mind is wandering, he's thinking about all those trips he's taken over the years."

I agreed that George probably was remembering previous travel experiences, but suggested that he also might be revealing that he was ready for a different journey—dying—and wanted to talk about it. Joan would have none of that, repeating that he was making no sense. She wouldn't even come into George's room with me.

I could see that Joan was emotionally exhausted. She'd buried two husbands after caring for them through illnesses similar to George's, and was taking refuge in the conviction that he didn't know what was happening or who was with him. This let her put some distance between herself and yet another brush with an emotionally painful experience. She agreed that it would be all right if I asked George what he meant, and if there was anything else he needed.

When I went into George's room, he seemed anxious, but greeted me as he usually did.

"How are you doing today?" I asked him.

"Well, I'm not eating much," George said. "I feel weaker, but I went out for a ride in the garden in my wheelchair, and the pain's not bothering me. But I can't find my passport. Do you know where my ticket is?"

"It sounds like you're planning to go somewhere," I answered. George nodded.

"Are you going on a journey?"

Nodding again, George said, "I don't have my papers."

"Are you talking about a different sort of journey?" I asked. "Maybe about leaving here? Maybe about dying?"

George responded to this suggestion with relief. He nodded, opened his mouth as if to speak, then shrugged.

"If you're talking about that journey, you don't need a passport and tickets," I said. "Are you wondering what you do need? Are you asking me what it will be like?"

This time he nodded more vigorously. He smiled and said, "Yes, I have to get ready."

I sat beside him and began to explain what he'd probably experience. Stopping frequently to make sure this was what he wanted to know, I described as simply as possible how his death would probably come. He'd continue to grow weaker, I explained. He might become so weak that he wouldn't be able to move, to talk, even to swallow—at which point his pain medicine would be given a different way—injection, suppository, or liquid under his tongue—rather than pills to swallow. His breathing would slow, become soft and quiet, then stop.

"Will it hurt?" he asked. "Will I suffer?"

No, I said. He'd move into light, warmth, and peace; none of this would cause him pain or fear. My words seemed to allay George's anxiety. I asked if there was anything he thought he needed to do to get ready for this journey.

"Joan doesn't know about passports and tickets," he said.

"Are you wondering if she understands that you're dying?" I asked.

George nodded in assent.

"I think she does," I said. "But I'll explain it to her again, if you want me to."

Again he nodded, smiled to me, and in an instant went back to discussing his changing appetite. He lived ten more days, sometimes asking about his passport or papers, but without distress. He seemed to be checking to see that all was in order, wanting to be sure that arrangements for his last journey were as smooth as possible, and that Joan was prepared for his departure.

Though she appreciated the support we gave her, Joan never could talk with George about death; however, she was at ease when someone else did so. She was able to show her love and concern for him by helping with his physical care.

Like Joan, some families have needs that prevent them from understanding or responding to a dying person's symbolic language. In such instances, others may need to intervene. Joan needed empathy and support; George needed information.

It may seem strange or cruel to say to someone who's dying, "I think you're going to die soon; this is what it's probably going to be like. . . ." But most dying people know they're dying. They aren't bothered by such openness; on the contrary, they welcome it. They're usually afraid, not of death and what comes after, but of what will happen before they die. They often want confirmation of the fact that they're dying, and a description of what it will be like for them. For those who seek this information, receiving it is less frightening than the unknown. In the same way, reassurance that their relatives know that death is coming, and are prepared for it, provides relief to the ones dying.

The following family was not only quick to grasp the concept of Nearing Death Awareness, but also excited by the opportunity to understand important messages from their dying husband and father.

PAUL

Elise described her husband as a "genius," and in many ways she wasn't exaggerating. A successful and respected aeronautical engineer, Paul was hired at an early age by NASA to work on various space shuttles.

"Paul always has a dozen projects going. He can fix or build anything. He loves being active," Elise said.

Because of his prostate cancer and the resulting severe weight loss, Paul had blood pressure so low that each time he tried to stand up it would fall even lower and he would faint. Consequently, he spent most of his time in bed, or in a reclining chair in his room. Despite various medications, we were unable to improve this condition.

"This just isn't his style. He won't put up with this for long," Elise said.

When Paul showed early signs of confusion, I explained the concept of Nearing Death Awareness to Elise and their daughters, aged twelve and sixteen. I suggested they listen carefully to everything that Paul said. They seemed fascinated and enthusiastic about it.

"We should be good at this. He's so smart, I've spent my life trying to figure out what the heck he's talking about!" Elise laughed.

Paul had a fascination with astronomy—especially lunar eclipses. And one was to take place in a few weeks. He spoke often of how much he wanted to witness it.

"Fix this damn blood pressure, so I can get on my feet to see it, okay? This might be my last chance to see one," he said.

But his blood pressure didn't improve enough for him to be more active. Realizing his request was futile, Paul became sullen and withdrawn, seeming to have lost interest in what was going on around him.

The day after the eclipse, his older daughter said, "Guess what? Dad dreamed about the eclipse last night. Even though he couldn't watch, he had lots to say about what it looked like and where it was. I told him it sounded like he had a ringside seat. He just smiled. My little sister said, 'Maybe he did!' "

A few days later, Elise called.

"I don't know—he seems weird today," she said. "But he won't tell us what's wrong!"

I agreed to come and check him. A quick physical examination indicated no significant changes, but his brows were furrowed with concentration. His normally peaceful demeanor had changed; he seemed busy, preoccupied, almost annoyed by our interruption.

"What's happening, Paul?" I asked. "Is something different?"

"I'm trying to figure out how I can take the house and everything in it!" he said.

"Take the house where?" I asked.

"With me!" he said, seeming irritated and indignant. Elise's eyes widened.

"Take the people in the house, too?" she asked.

"Of course!" he said.

"Is there anything we can do to help?" I asked.

"No, I have to do this by myself!" he said. Then he rolled over on his side and went to sleep.

In the kitchen I asked Elise and the girls what they thought this all meant.

"I'm glad he saw the eclipse, 'cause he really wanted to," his younger daughter said.

"Maybe he doesn't want to leave us or this house. Did you know that he built it himself?" the older daughter asked. We agreed that was possible.

Over the next week, Paul spoke to his family often and in great detail about his plans for taking his family and his house with him when he died—he'd dig up the foundation, seal off the water and gas lines, store food, and build a self-contained heating system.

Then one day Elise found Paul very quiet, having little to say.

"What's the matter, Paul?" she asked. "You're so quiet! Is something wrong?" His eyes filled with tears.

"It's neither practical nor possible," he said.

"I know," she said, holding him close.

"But we'll never forget how hard you tried," she went on tearfully. "We'll work together to take care of each other and your beautiful house. We love you and we're going to miss you. It'll be hard without you, but we'll be okay."

From that conversation on, Paul stopped speaking. His only responses were a nod or shake of his head, but he seemed very peaceful. By the next day, he'd slipped quietly into a coma; a few hours later, with Elise and the girls at his bedside, he died.

At his funeral, Elise and the girls told the story to some of Paul's coworkers.

"Isn't it just like Paul to try to do the impossible?" Elise said with a chuckle. "If anybody could have figured out a way to take his family and his house with him, it would have been Paul!"

The gift of sharing, love, and concern Paul had given his family already was helping them deal with their loss and grief.

The way the messages in this chapter were offered reflects the personalities and experiences of the senders. Some messages are long, detailed, and stated often. Others are brief and fleeting. Some are obscure, others are crystal clear. All gave the message "I'm getting ready to leave."

Dick, who loved boats, simply asked once about the tide as he prepared for his last voyage, while engineer Paul dove into the complex and ultimately insoluble problem of taking his family and house with him.

George, ever the precise military man, reminded those around him of his need for his papers and passport.

At the core of each such message is the news that dying people know they are dying—perhaps before anyone else. Instead of anxiety, that knowledge may be accompanied by a need for information about the process of dying or concern for those they love. Simple, brief, and concise information helps to allay those fears. The family's reassurances—that they'll be all right and they know what's going on—often bring the peace a dying person needs. If possible, such comfort should come directly from the family; if impossible, a third party can—and should—attempt to reassure and comfort the individual.

CHAPTER SEVEN

BEING IN THE PRESENCE OF SOMEONE NOT ALIVE: "I'M NOT ALONE."

The most prevalent theme in Nearing Death Awareness seems to be the presence of someone not alive. The timing varies; the experience can happen hours or days or sometimes weeks before the actual death.

Dying people often interact with someone invisible to others—talking to them, smiling or nodding at them. Sometimes, more than one invisible person is involved.

The unseen person's identity often is clear to the dying. Generally they recognize someone significant from their lives—parent, spouse, sibling, friend—who is already dead. There is often a sense of pleasure, even of joyful reunion, in seeing that person again. Some see religious figures—angels, perhaps, or spirits. Even when people don't recognize the figure they're seeing they don't appear upset or frightened. Most accept these other presences without question.

Professional background and training is not a requirement for listening to and understanding these special messages. Because family and friends know intimately a person's personality and life experience, they are often best qualified to find hidden messages. A friend from New England told us the following story:

STEVE

A sharp young man with a well-developed sense of humor, Steve was the youngest in a large, fun-loving Boston family. Until he started his professional career, each summer was spent at the family's beach house on Cape Cod. There he became fast friends with Ralph, his next-door neighbor, whose family came each summer from Ohio. Both were avid swimmers; Steve's mother called them "the Devilish Duo," as their summers were full of activity and pranks.

Both boys graduated from college and established themselves in good careers, but sadly that was the end of their carefree summers together. They rarely got to see each other, and apart from Christmas cards, didn't correspond.

A tragic automobile accident left Steve paralyzed from the neck down at the age of twenty-seven. After he had spent many months in the hospital, then more in a rehabilitation facility, his family decided to try to care for him at home, but within two months became exhausted by his twenty-four-hour needs. With heavy hearts and a terrible sense of failure, they placed him in a nursing home.

Through all of this, Steve hadn't lost his sense of humor. Despite being unable to do anything for himself, he threatened to run away if the nurses didn't spoil him.

"But it was easy to spoil Steve," one nurse told his mother. "He liked to be in his wheelchair in the hall so he could be in the middle of everything. He was such a nut—he kept us all laughing! When one of the patients was upset or depressed, we'd push Steve in to visit, and he was so good with the new patients we called him 'the welcome wagon man'!"

Unfortunately, as is common with quadriplegics like Steve, pneumonia developed, which didn't respond to treatment. Steve died. His family was devastated and a wave of grief rippled through the nursing home.

Weeks later a letter arrived with an Ohio postmark. The correspondent identified herself as Ralph's widow. She was writing to say that Ralph had died recently of cancer. Ralph hadn't known of Steve's paralysis or death. However, in the last few weeks before he died, Ralph began to have visions. Initially his wife dismissed it as confusion. Just before he died—and just after Steve had died—Ralph sat up.

"Oh, look!" he said excitedly. "Here comes Steve! He's come to take me swimming."

Steve's family took great comfort in that letter and the thought that somewhere Steve was whole again, doing what he loved.

"The 'Devilish Duo' are up to their old pranks again!" Steve's mother said. And Ralph's widow took comfort in knowing that her husband's boyhood friend had truly come for him; he hadn't died alone.

It's interesting to note that this story reaffirms what has been reported in other literature—the belief that in the next life we are whole and perfect, regardless of our physical limitations or losses in this life.

FRED

Fred, his wife, Ann, and their only child, Ruth, were a close family. Ann and Fred were in their eighties; Ruth, forty-seven, lived with them. Fred was dying of prostate cancer that had spread to his bones and lungs. Despite her age, Ann was able to take care of him at home, with a great deal of assistance from Ruth.

Fred was mentally alert, but his body was failing. He continued to live longer than seemed possible. This was very hard on Ann; she realized Fred was ready to die, and couldn't understand why he didn't. It also was hard on Ruth; besides feeling sad that her father was so ill, she worried about how long she and her mother could continue to take care of him.

One day I asked Ann if she thought Fred might be hanging on because he was worried about how she'd manage without him.

"That's very likely," Ann said.

"How do you feel about discussing this with him?" I asked.

"That makes sense to me," Ann said. "But I don't know what to say. Would you come and help me?"

Ann called Ruth and we went into the bedroom. They sat on either side of Fred, holding hands with one another and with him.

"Fred, are you afraid of dying?" Ann asked.

"No," he said.

"Are you worried about anything?"

"I'm worried about how you'll get by after I'm gone," he said. He tried to smile at her, but his eyes were anxious.

"Now, don't be afraid to go," Ann said. "I'm going to miss you terribly, but I'll be all right. And you know it won't be long before I'll be joining you."

For more than an hour the three sat, speaking of many things. They talked of Ann and Fred's lives together, how they'd met on the beach and fallen in love, how Ann had converted to Fred's faith, Judaism, and how important their religion had been through the years. They talked of the joy they'd experienced raising Ruth, and the love all three shared. Interspersed among these tender reminiscences were Fred's practical directions to Ann about how she should take care of things and get on with her life after he died.

At one point Fred sat up and waved his hand excitedly, as if brushing away an interruption. Periodically he'd break off the conversation to look across the room, as if seeing someone we could not see. Once, he turned his head again and said impatiently, "Would you wait, I'm not ready yet!"

Soon after, having talked of his concern for Ann, given her advice, and listened to her reassurances that she'd manage without him, Fred kissed Ann and Ruth good-bye, leaned back against the pillow, took a few quiet breaths, and died.

Fred did not say in so many words, "There are others in the room," but he certainly behaved as if that were the case. His manner implied that he knew who they were, and that he was neither surprised nor frightened—only impatient, as if they were trying to rush him. Neither were Ann and Ruth startled by Fred's gestures and statements; they assumed he was talking with people he'd loved who would be accompanying him on his journey.

• • •

Very often family and friends don't know who the dying person is seeing because they don't ask. Sometimes the one dying doesn't know either, but doesn't seem to find this distressing.

MARTHA

Martha was in her early sixties; dying of uterine cancer, which had spread throughout her pelvis. A widow, she'd lived for many years with her daughter and family.

Martha's experience with unseen people was not very dramatic, but her reaction was typical. She wasn't at all surprised or upset by it, and was even able to express her pleasure at seeing what no one else could see.

Several weeks before she died, Martha said to me, "Do you know who the little girl is?"

"Which little girl?" I asked.

"You know, the one who comes to see me," she said. "The one the others can't see."

Martha described several visitors unseen by others. She knew most of them—her parents and sisters, all of whom were dead—but couldn't identify a child who appeared with them. That didn't bother her.

"Don't worry," she told me, "I'll figure it out before I go, or I'll find out when I get there. Have you seen them?"

"No, I haven't," I said. "But I believe that you do. Are they here now?"

"They left a little while ago," Martha said. "They don't stay all the time; they just come and go."

"What is it like when they're here?" I asked.

"Well, sometimes we talk, but usually I just know that they're here," Martha said. "I know that they love me, and that they'll be here with me when it's time."

"When it's time . . . ?"

"When I die," Martha said matter-of-factly.

. . .

In most cases the people seen are dead relatives or friends, but sometimes people will tell of seeing an angel, or God, or some other religious figure. One man said he'd seen the Lord's face; another said, "There was an angel standing by my bed." Neither of them, nor any of the other people who reported seeing these spiritual beings, were upset. They usually were calm as they talked about it, and seemed comforted and more peaceful in the presence of their invisible visitors.

We wondered if people spoke about spiritual or religious beings because they were conditioned to expect them by their religious beliefs—particularly if the person believed in a life after death. We also were concerned that we might be projecting our own beliefs and expectations onto these situations. Because of our concerns we were particularly interested in the following situation.

ANGELA

Angela was a delightful musician, dying of melanoma at twenty-five. When she entered the hospice inpatient unit, her parents, three younger brothers, and several close friends seemed to move in with her. Her parents took turns spending the night in her room; during the day a small crowd gathered there.

The melanoma had started as a mole on her arm, then spread. Many of her more incapacitating symptoms resulted from its effect on her brain. Her left side was paralyzed; she was blind and too weak to get out of bed. But Angela still could speak and was by no means helpless. The day she was admitted to the unit, she said firmly, "I know about you hospice people; I don't want any of that spiritual stuff, no prayers, no chaplains. That's not my thing! I'm an atheist. I don't believe in God or Heaven."

The staff respected Angela's position, but her mother found it very difficult. A devout Catholic, she couldn't accept her daughter's rejection of God and the faith she'd been raised in.

"All the other kids believe in God and go to church," the mother said. "We don't know what happened with Angela! We raised them all the same, but it never took with her."

One dark, chilly February morning, I responded to Angela's call bell. Her mother had spent the night, and she stirred on her cot as I pushed open the door.

"Hi, Angela, what can I do for you?" I said.

"Did someone come in here to see me?" she said.

"I don't think so, I didn't see anyone. It's not even dawn yet, and there's no one around," I said. "Why do you ask?"

"I saw an angel."

I sat on the bed.

"Tell me what happened," I said.

"When I woke up there was an angel sitting in the light from the window," Angela said, with a smile on her face. She described feeling very drawn toward this being, who exuded warmth, love, and caring.

Her mother jumped off the cot.

"Angela, it's a sign from God!" she said.

"Mother, I don't believe in God!" Angela said, now exasperated.

"That doesn't matter," her mother said. "You've seen God, or at least a messenger from God!"

"Does it matter who it is?" Angela snapped. "Isn't it enough to know that there's someone so loving and caring waiting for me?"

"Angela, what do you think it means?" I asked.

"I don't believe in angels or God, but someone was here with me. Whoever it was loves me and is waiting for me. So it means I won't die alone," she said, the smile returning to her face. Her mother's eyes filled with tears, and she put her arms around her daughter.

"Darling, it doesn't matter who it is," she said. "I'm just so pleased this happened!"

Later, outside Angela's room, her mother said, "I know it was either God or an angel, and she insists it can't be—you know how stubborn she can be. But what matters is that this happened; it's not important what we call the person!" She had realized her daughter's fear of the loneliness of death was alleviated by the knowledge of that loving presence waiting for her.

Dying people may not be upset by encountering presences unseen by others, but such visitations can unsettle family members, friends, and some health-care professionals. "Now, you know Mother's been dead for years," a son may say to his dying father. "You can't possibly have seen her!" Or the response may be "You must be dreaming; maybe it's your medicines."

These comments don't help; on the contrary, they usually discourage the dying from sharing more of their experiences, and may lead to bewilderment.

A common misinterpretation of dying people's messages about unseen presences is that they must be hallucinating as a result of medicines. This can lead well-meaning onlookers to suggest potentially disastrous changes in a patient's medication regimen.

PETE

Before Pete was admitted to the hospice program, his major problem was pain. A large, gruff man, he prided himself on his toughness.

"I don't believe in pills," he'd said.

His usual pattern was to resist taking any pain medicine. When his pain increased to the point that he couldn't stand it, he'd take a dose of medicine—which wouldn't work because the pain was, by then, so intense. So he'd take another—sometimes as many as three or four—before getting any relief. The accumulated doses would then make him sleepy and disoriented, which increased his dislike of medicines.

When Pete came into our program we taught him to use small, regular doses of medicine, every four hours. This brought his pain under control, helping Pete to enjoy six months of comfortable time.

However, when Pete mentioned to his sister he'd been talking to their brother, John, she grew concerned—John had been dead for more than ten years. A neighbor who was present said Pete was hallucinating as a result of his medicines, and urged that he stop taking them. Pete's sister called me. I visited to assess Pete's condition, and explained that the medicines were not causing these visions. I suggested that Pete was in fact seeing John; the sister had no difficulty accepting it.

"John was the oldest, he'd want to keep an eye on his brother," she said, adding that it helped her to know that someone else from the family would be with Pete as he died, and afterward.

The neighbor's advice could have caused a loss of pain control and brought Pete a great deal of suffering.

Sometimes a family decides to withhold information about the death of someone the dying person knows. This impulse to spare someone emotional pain is laudable, but the truth often helps bring peace, not discomfort.

S U

A dignified Chinese woman, Su was getting devoted care from her daughter, Lily. Both were Buddhists, and very accepting of the mother's terminal status.

"I've had a good life for ninety-three years," she said. "And I've been on this earth long enough!" She dreamed often of her husband, who had died some years before.

"I will join him soon," she said.

But one day Su seemed very puzzled.

"Why is my sister with my husband?" she asked. "They are both calling me to come."

"Is your sister dead?" I asked.

"No, she still lives in China," she said. "I have not seen her for many years."

When I related this conversation to the daughter, she was astonished and tearful.

"My aunt died two days ago in China," Lily said. "We decided not to tell Mother—her sister had the same kind of cancer. It was a very painful death; she lived in a remote village where good medical care wasn't available. We didn't want to upset or frighten Mother, since she is so sick herself."

"What do you think about your mother's questioning why she is being called to come by both her sister and your father?" I asked.

"Mother tells me that my father's been calling her to be with him for the past week," Lily said. "It gives me comfort to know they will be together again in the next life. So I guess her sister is waiting there for her also," Lily said after much thought.

"Do you think the news of her sister's death will upset your mother?"

"No, I guess not—they loved each other a great deal. So it'll be wonderful for them all to be together again. I guess I should tell her the truth."

When Lily tearfully told her mother about her sister's illness and death, Su said, with a knowing smile, "Now I understand." Her puzzle solved, she died three weeks later, at peace and with a sense of anticipation.

The companionship and support these presences provide for a person about to die is evident. But some terminally ill people have these experiences months before their deaths and benefit in a similar way over a longer period of time.

PEGGY

Peggy, a young woman dying of lymphoma that had advanced to the point where she was very weak, slept most of the time and was sometimes slightly confused.

When our colleague arrived for a routine visit, Peggy called out in a strong, clear voice.

"Come on up, I'm upstairs!" she said. She looked bright, radiant, and was unusually active.

"How are you?" the nurse asked. "You look particularly beautiful today."

"Let me tell you what happened to me," Peggy said. "I was lying here in bed yesterday, sort of drifting in and out of sleep, and remembering back to a happy time in my childhood. My brother and I were taken in by my aunt during a time that my parents were having financial difficulty. I really loved my aunt; she was wonderful—so loving to both of us. It was just a very happy time for me. I still love her a lot. I woke up with a start when I felt a warm, caring hand on my shoulder. I looked around behind me and there was my aunt smiling at me as she touched me. It made me feel so good and safe."

"Where is your aunt?" the nurse asked.

"She lives in Massachusetts," Peggy said. "I haven't seen her in a long time because she's sick. But I felt her with me off and on all day; it made me feel so good! Last night my uncle called to say she died yesterday—and at the same time that I was first aware of her being with me! And then today I woke up and she was touching me again!"

"What a nice experience," the nurse said. "I can see how good it's made you feel. What do you think it means?"

"That she'll be there for me when I die," Peggy replied with a radiant smile. "And we'll be together again."

Peggy recognized her aunt, and said clearly who she saw. Sometimes the communication may be a little less clear.

LEONA

Leona was semiconscious and Ray was distraught.

"It's so unfair," he said. "She always tried to help other people and now she can't do anything for herself. She stood by our son Chuck when he had trouble with drugs, and it nearly broke her heart when our daughter, Jo Beth, died."

I asked about Jo Beth. Ray explained that she'd been the light of their lives—smart, well liked, and the very image of her mother when it came to helping others.

"When she was still in high school, a deaf family moved into the block. The neighbors were sort of standoffish, but Leona and Jo Beth took a course in sign language so they could talk to the new people. The two of them used to practice their signing all the time. They bugged me and Chuck to learn, too, but all we ever managed were a few easy ones," Ray said, holding up his left hand in a gesture. "That means 'I love you.' Jo Beth would tease us that if we wouldn't learn we couldn't gripe about her and Mom and their 'secret language.' "

Ray went on to describe how Jo Beth had died. In her freshman year at college in a neighboring state, she'd come down with appendicitis. During emergency surgery she reacted badly to the anesthesia and her heart stopped. She was resuscitated but the resulting lack of oxygen damaged her brain, leaving her in a coma like the one that now entrapped Leona.

"For weeks we prayed that she'd wake up and be all right," Ray said. "Finally she did come out of it, but she couldn't talk or do anything for herself, and she didn't seem to know us. It nearly killed her mother, and her brother kept saying it should have been him. The family sort of came apart.

"Eventually we got Jo Beth into a nursing home; she lived another eighteen months, but she never got better. Leona visited every day, sitting and talking to Jo Beth as if she could understand. After she died, Leona got involved with a group that works with people in situations like ours; she said she wanted to make something positive out of our pain."

Weeks passed, Leona neared death in peace and comfort. Chuck flew in from the West Coast. They sat with Leona and talked to her, as she had done so often with a comatose Jo Beth years before.

In the moments before her death, Leona seemed to awaken. She opened her eyes and looked past Ray and Chuck, breaking into a radiant smile. She moved her hand, then closed her eyes and died.

"Dad, look what she did with her right hand!" Chuck said.

"She signed 'I love you' the way she always did with Jo Beth."
The father hugged his son. "They're together again," he said.

We can best respond to people who experience the presence of someone not alive by expecting it to happen. Such messages usually aren't hard to understand. Often a person will say clearly, "My father was here," or "There's someone warm and caring waiting for me." If you accept these messages you can then try to understand what the person is telling you, rather than looking for other explanations, such as medicine, hallucination, or loss of intellectual function.

Don't argue about what's real. Speak only the truth, but don't try to persuade someone that what he or she is seeing is unreal. Suppose a dying person asks, "Do you know where John is? He was here earlier." Say, "Remember—John died a few years ago." This provides the information you were asked for, and sets up the next phase of conversation. But attempting to "humor" the person with "Yes, dear, of course, he's in the other room" is condescending and false. A flat denial that John could be present—"You can't possibly have seen John; he's been dead for ten years"—will bewilder the one dying, who may stop trying to communicate with you. No matter what you know to be true, the person *has* seen John, won't believe that he hasn't, and may wonder why you're trying to talk him out of it.

It's also counterproductive to withhold information about another's death. It's a kind thought, but truth often helps bring peace, not discomfort.

If you can't comprehend what a dying person means, ask gently; if the person is willing or able to talk about it, you may learn more.

The most important thing to remember when a dying person sees someone invisible to you is that death is not lonely. Many people fear that they, or someone they love, will die alone. In fact, what the stories of these people tell us is that they didn't die alone, and neither will we. Those who have died before us, or some spiritual beings, will be companions on our journey.

CHAPTER EIGHT

SEEING A PLACE: "I SEE WHERE I'M GOING."

Many dying people tell of seeing a place not visible to anyone else. Their descriptions are brief—rarely exceeding a sentence or two—and not very specific, but usually glowing. They may describe the place as beautiful or lovely, but the response to "Tell me more . . ." often is a dreamy look and a shake of the head or several false starts and then: "I can't."

Even so a glimpse of this other place seems to bring peace, comfort, and security to the dying person—reactions shared by those able to listen and understand.

BOBBY

Bobby, thirty-two, was being cared for in the home of his older brother Bill. Incontinent, his skin yellow with jaundice, Bobby had lost so much weight that his once-strong body was reduced to skin stretched tightly over jutting bones. Bill and their sister Mary would bath Bobby in bed, brush his teeth, rub his back, and do everything else necessary to keep him comfortable.

Bobby couldn't swallow, so we taught Bill and Mary to inject his pain medicine, and to keep his mouth moist by frequent cleansing with soft sponges.

Bobby also had difficulty speaking. Dying people can become

so weak that even a whisper demands more effort and energy than they can muster.

One day, thinking his brother might be in pain but unable to communicate it, Bill called the hospice office.

When I arrived, I found Bobby uncomfortable and anxious. In addition to checking his blood pressure, pulse, breathing rate, and lung function, I needed to ask Bobby some questions. Because he was unable to speak I tried an alternative method of gathering information.

"I'm going to ask you some questions, Bobby," I said. "I want you to blink your eyes once if the answer is 'yes' and twice if the answer is 'no.' Do you understand?"

Bobby blinked once.

"Are you in pain?"

"No," he blinked in response.

"You seem anxious to me, are you?"

"Yes."

"Are you afraid?"

"Yes."

"Would you like me to explain what's happening to you?"

"Yes."

Even as he blinked his response, the anxiety seemed to begin to ease. Speaking slowly and pausing frequently to ask if this was what he wanted to know, I told Bobby that he seemed to be getting weaker, and that soon he'd become weaker still. He might not be able to open his eyes or respond to us at all, although he'd continue to hear what was going on.

"Your breathing will get quieter and slower . . ." I said.

". . . and then you'll just go quietly home to Jesus," Bill said, jumping into our conversation.

Bobby looked at his brother, then at me—a question in his eyes. When I nodded in agreement, he smiled. I added that his death would be quiet, easy, peaceful, and with no pain. Bobby smiled again, closed his eyes, and relaxed into the pillows.

From then on he rested quietly, with Bill and Mary beside him, talking softly. Occasionally he'd open his eyes and smile at them.

Because their brother was too weak to speak, Bill and Mary

thought pain was causing his agitation. He *was* experiencing pain—emotional pain. The solution to it was not medicine but information and reassurance about what was happening. My explanation, along with his siblings' caring presence, relieved much of Bobby's anxiety.

Bobby's pain medicine was due, so I offered to give it. I left the room and returned with a syringe.

"Can I rearrange your pillows and give you a shot to keep the pain away?" I asked.

Bobby blinked once.

As I put my arm around his shoulder, his breathing changed, pausing for several seconds, then starting again.

"His breathing is changing," I said to Bill and Mary. "I think he's going."

Bill called other family members from elsewhere in the house. They gathered around the bed. Bobby's breathing changed again. Several times it slowed, stopped for many seconds at a time, then started again.

Mary clung tightly to Bobby, pleading with him not to leave her. Bill, stroking his brother's cheek, said, "You go right home to Jesus, Bobby." Around the bed, the others were telling Bobby they loved him and would miss him.

Finally, with one last, long sigh, Bobby died. As we sat—holding him and one another—Bill said that, when I had gone to get the medicine, Bobby had spoken clearly for the first time in more than three days.

"He told us, 'I can see the light down the road and it's beautiful,' " Bill said.

This glimpse of the other place gives immeasurable comfort to many, and often is perceived as a final gift from the one who died.

"I've never been a religious person, but being there when Bobby died was a real spiritual experience," his sister said later. "I'll never be the same again."

Bill echoed her sentiments at the funeral. "Because Bobby's death was so peaceful, I'll never be as scared of death," he said.

"He gave me a little preview of what lay beyond it for him, and, I hope, for me."

Interpretations of statements about another place depend on what, if anything, people believe about an afterlife. Most interpret "seeing another place" as a sign that life will continue after death. More specific interpretations depend upon individual beliefs. Raised a Christian, Bobby hadn't wanted to see any clergy, but after he died Bill asked for a priest, who came while Bobby's body still lay in the bedroom. Bill and Mary explained how their brother had died, and what he'd said.

"What do you think he was telling you?" the priest asked.

"He must have been seeing Heaven," Bill said.

"Our Christian faith is based on the suffering, death, and resurrection of Jesus," the priest said. "You've witnessed your brother's suffering and death, and he gave you a glimpse of his resurrection."

Then, with everyone holding hands around Bobby, he offered a prayer for Bobby's eternal peace and for the strength and comfort of those who loved him.

The timing of Bobby's description of the other place isn't unusual. Often it is among a dying person's final statements, and is seen as a sign that death is imminent. But some dying people see this place days, weeks, or even months before death. And others interpret the vision differently than Bobby's family did.

LYNN

Asked about her religious affiliation, Lynn, an economist, said, "I don't have any religion. I've never believed in God or anything like that, I'm just not interested."

Seven weeks before her death, she told me, "I had a dream, but it wasn't really a dream—I was in such a lovely place."

She wouldn't, or couldn't, go on, except to say she'd seen where she was going.

"I know it wasn't a dream, it was so lovely," she said more

than once. Then she'd shake her head, smile, and shrug. She seemed comforted by what she'd seen and often wore a dreamy half-smile and a distant look in her eyes.

"You seem to be far away," I said.

"It's not so far," Lynn said. "And it's so lovely."

Lynn's daughter, Sandra, reacted by asking if her mother was taking too much medicine. We assured her that this wasn't the case; Lynn was taking few medicines, and in small doses. We encouraged Sandra to talk more with her mother about the dream that wasn't a dream.

"She knows she's dying, but now she seems to know that she will somehow continue to exist afterward," Sandra said. "Mother's always maintained that people simply cease to exist after death, but now she's seen somewhere new. She says there's a place you go after death. I doubt that there is, but I find myself wondering if she's right."

Months after Lynn's peaceful death, Sandra said it had been disturbing to confront her mother's changed ideas about the afterlife. But she also found the experience liberating.

"I still don't believe any of those religious stories, but I no longer believe that when I die I'll just come to an end," Sandra said. "What I learned from my mother is that in some way *we do* continue after death, and I'm still trying to figure out what that existence might be like." It comforted her to think that her mother still existed somehow and that they might see one another again.

Sandra's interpretation of her mother's seeing another place differs from the interpretation that Bobby's family made. But the variance is in the details, not the essence: that life will continue after death.

When people like Bobby and Lynn see another place as part of their Nearing Death Awareness, they do not seem to experience leaving their bodies: rather they remain in the bodies and are aware of two existences. In an out-of-body experience people report leaving their bodies, going elsewhere, looking back or down at their bodies, and may speak of things they couldn't otherwise have seen or heard.

L U C Y

Near dawn, a patient's daughter telephoned.

"Mother says she's been out of her body and has been somewhere else, but now she's back and keeps wanting to tell me about it," Ellie said in a tight, breathless voice. "Would you please come over?"

"How is she now?" I asked.

"She says she's fine," Ellie said.

"Does she seem any different to you?"

"No, she's the same as always, except for this story of leaving her body."

"Is she upset by having left her body?"

"No, she's fine, feeling quite comfortable, and asking for a cup of coffee."

I told Ellie to make the coffee; I'd be right over.

When I arrived, Ellie looked shaken; her mother was serene.

"How are you doing?" I asked Lucy.

"I was just telling Ellie that I went out of here and left this old body behind for a while," Lucy said.

"Where did you go?" I asked.

"Back to the old farm in Pennsylvania where I grew up," she said. "The kitchen looked the same, and the view across the fields where the cows used to be was so fresh and green."

Lucy talked at length about the old farmhouse, how she'd lived in it until she was nearly twenty, then she'd continued to visit until the death of the uncle who owned it. After it was sold, she hadn't returned. In her opinion she'd been transported to a place she particularly loved.

"What do you think this means?" I asked Lucy.

"Oh, I don't know, I guess I just wanted to see it again."

. . .

In describing her out-of-body experience, Lucy gave many specific details. In contrast, when people with Nearing Death Awareness describe another place, they're usually very brief, as well as very vague. Sometimes they only refer to a light.

EMMA

Emma, fifty, had a husband, and two children in their early twenties. When I asked Emma what she missed most, because of the limitations of her illness, she replied, "Entertaining—I love to give parties and cook wonderful food for my family and friends."

Her husband reported that many friends brought food to them now, always hoping to send just the right thing to tempt Emma's disappearing appetite. So Emma knew that her family were still eating very well, despite the fact that she could no longer cook for them. But it was the joy of sharing her creative cooking with the people she loved that she missed so much.

Her daughter was about to graduate from college, and Emma spoke often about how she looked forward to seeing her daughter in a cap and gown. "She's the first college graduate in our family!" she said proudly.

As her illness progressed, Emma spent more time in bed. About a month before she died I visited, and found her propped up on pillows staring into space with a dreamy look in her eyes. She was smiling peacefully.

"What's happening, Emma?" I asked.

"There's that beautiful light," she whispered softly. Despite my gentle questioning, she continued to smile dreamily, but offered no further information. She mentioned the "light" two or three times during my next few visits, never providing details but continuing to look radiant and peaceful.

She was a strong-willed woman, who struggled to deal with her increasing loss of control as she became sicker. She insisted on continuing to manage her own medicines despite the fact that she was sometimes slightly confused. Her family and nurses were very concerned about her safety and felt this might be dangerous, yet she could not relinquish this control. Rather than have a private-duty nurse at home, Emma chose to be admitted into the hospice unit. I visited her shortly after she was admitted.

"Oh, if only I could relax!" she complained.

"What would happen if you relaxed?" I said.

"Well, that light would come closer and I could get to know all these people." For a split second I thought she was referring to her roommates or the staff on the unit.

Unsure, I asked, "What people?"

Emma looked surprised, as if I were asking a ridiculous question.

"All these people around my bed, of course!" she said, waving her arm to show the size of the crowd I couldn't see.

"You will relax," I reassured her. "This is a safe place to relax, and a safe place to get to know all these people around you. The beautiful light will come closer and everything will be all right."

The nurse assigned to Emma's care reported that she was comfortable but deteriorating, and often appeared busy—preoccupied, as though giving directions or fussing at people unseen.

On the eve of her daughter's graduation, I visited again and asked, "What's happening, Emma?"

"Well, I have so much to do with all these people! And that light just keeps coming closer!" she replied with a trace of annoyance.

"Do you know any of these people?" I asked her.

"Well, there's my father," she said, squinting as if to see him better. I smiled and nodded, knowing that her father had died less than a year before.

"Is he waiting for you?" I asked.

She looked surprised. "For heaven's sake, is *that* what he's doing?" she asked.

"Emma, when will your work be done?" I continued with mounting curiosity.

"Oh, I think probably Sunday," she answered. I immediately called her family to alert them.

The next day, Emma put on her wig and makeup to prepare

for her daughter's visit after graduation. It was quite a celebration, with cake, champagne, and lots of family pictures taken.

The next morning Emma again put on her wig and makeup,
lay back against the pillows with a contented sigh, and within
a few hours had slipped from sleep into a brief coma. With her
family quietly sitting around her, she peacefully died. As she
had predicted, it was Sunday and her work was done.

We don't know what Emma saw that she described as the light.
But others have told of "a place of light and warmth" or "a
person full of light." The descriptions are vague, but the emotions evoked by these experiences are clear: comfort and peace.

Maybe the descriptions are vague because people feel they
are trying to describe the indescribable. A coworker who had a
Near Death Experience said, "I can tell you what happened,
but I really can't explain what it was like; words are just in-
adequate." She told us of another experience and agreed with
this patient's explanation of why we don't hear more.

CLARE

Clare, twenty-three, had just started work as a second-grade
teacher when she began to develop headaches. Busy learning
her new job, she ignored them. Over the winter she had several colds; this happens to many new teachers, but these
colds seemed particularly persistent. In December she caught
the flu.

At spring break her mother pushed her to see a doctor. Clare
was diagnosed with acute leukemia, and told she probably would
die within weeks.

The prognosis was wrong. An experimental treatment put the
disease into remission. Clare had to resign from her teaching
position, but found another way to work with children. Between
her frequent hospital stays she volunteered as a tutor at a children's hospital.

But five years later time began to run out; Clare moved home with her parents, and was referred for hospice care.

On the piano that she sometimes still played, I saw photos of Clare as she had been—young and healthy, with a mane of thick red hair—at the beach, riding a bike, playing softball. Now her hair was a few wisps over a bony scalp, her body wasted and weak, and her cheeks bloated.

She spent her days in a wheelchair or on the living-room couch. Her mother, also a teacher, had taken an extended leave of absence to take care of Clare. She made a fine nurse, and was able to respond helpfully to what Clare called her "roller-coaster" moods.

Many people with serious illnesses know the ups and downs of which Clare spoke. On "up" days treatments seem to be working, cure or remission seems not only possible but imminent, and there is a feeling of elation, excitement, and anticipation.

"But on days when a treatment isn't working, or I've got so many side effects that it feels like it's going to kill me faster than the cancer—those are the real 'downs,' " Clare said. "It feels like I'm speeding downhill completely out of control. I even get the same kind of feelings inside that I used to get on a roller-coaster when I was a kid. Going up is exciting but scary, because I know how far down I might fall. And the downhill ride is a combination of fear and nausea as I wait for the crash that I know will happen."

Her brother Sam was Clare's other pillar of support. Three years older, he was energetic and witty. When Sam was around, the affectionate teasing never stopped.

One day Clare showed me a copy of Kenneth Ring's book, *Heading Toward Omega,* which explores the effect on values and behavior of having a Near Death Experience.

"Sam brought this," she said. "He wants me to read it, but it sounds kind of weird. He suggested I ask you what you think. Is it worth reading?"

Having read and enjoyed the book, I told her I'd found it fascinating and thought she might find it helpful; I said I'd be happy to talk about it with her.

On my next visit Clare said she'd read the book, but had some questions: Did I think those stories were true? Could the people have made them up? Maybe they were on drugs, legal or otherwise?

"Ring and others have researched hundreds of people's experiences," I said. "Doesn't he answer those questions right in the book?"

"Yes," said Clare with a grin. "I wanted to see what you thought. I almost believe it but I'm still a little skeptical. I've never met anyone who's had an experience like that, have you?"

"Yes," I said. "I had one."

"Oh, wow," she exclaimed. "What happened?

"When I was a teenager, I nearly drowned," I said. "I was at the beach and was caught in a current. When they dragged me out they thought I was dead, but someone resuscitated me."

"And you had some kind of experience while that was going on?" Clare asked. "Would you mind telling me about it?"

"I was out swimming and got a cramp. At first I thought I could float until it went away, but the current was stronger than I thought," I said. "So I screamed for help. No one heard me. A wave took me under and I panicked. I was going up and down, being pulled farther and farther out. It was awful. I was choking, my lungs felt like they would burst. I wasn't even coming up above the surface; when I opened my mouth I'd take in more water, and I knew I was going to die.

"Suddenly, much faster than I can tell you, everything changed. My panic disappeared. I wasn't struggling to breathe; I was completely relaxed and peaceful, surrounded by a warm, bright light. It enveloped me and somehow I became part of it. I didn't see anyone, but I felt God's presence. I knew I was dying and it was perfectly all right."

I stopped, my eyes filling with tears. Clare took my hand.

"Does it upset you to talk about it?" she asked.

"No, it's not upsetting," I said. "But when I talk about it I can remember everything so vividly it's almost as if I'm there again. It was such a powerful experience. . . ."

I wiped my eyes and thanked her for the tissues she'd passed me.

"I've never dried your tears before," she said. "Usually that's what you do for me. Thank you for telling me that. Can you tell me what you think it all means?"

"Everything changed when I stopped breathing. At that moment I was dying and going from this life to the next one. The light was God, and I felt peaceful and loved."

"Is that what will happen to me?" Clare asked.

I told her I thought her experience would be similar, but not quite the same. I said I thought she'd have a more gradual, prolonged experience, with some awareness of being both places at once.

Two months later Clare died. In her final week, drained of energy, she often seemed to be looking through people. Sam asked me if I thought she might be seeing something or someone. He'd asked her and received no reply, just a slight smile.

"Clare, what are you seeing?" I asked.

"It's that place, *you* know, you were there," she said.

"Clare, what's it like?" Sam said, putting a hand on her cheek. "You've got to tell me."

Clare snuggled against her brother's hand and smiled.

"I can't," she said. "You'll have to wait your turn."

Maybe Clara's answer to Sam is the answer for all of us: until it's our turn to die, we can't know. But until then we can listen to, learn from, and be comforted by people who see and try to tell us.

Sometimes comments about the other place are easy to miss or hard to understand. Often people mention a place or express a wish to go home, even when they *are* home. In that case, ask "Which home?" If someone seems to be saying death will be soon, ask, "Are you telling me you're about to go to this other place?" or "Do you mean you're ready to leave?" With some people you can speak directly, "Are you saying you'll be dying soon?"

When a dying person mentions another place, ask gently if they'd like to tell you about it. You may or may not hear much, but you'll learn something. Dying people teach us that there may be some continuation of life beyond death. As dying people drift in and out of the other place, they assure us of its existence, its beauty, and its peace.

CHAPTER NINE

KNOWING WHEN DEATH WILL OCCUR: "IT WILL BE WHEN..."

Dying people often seem to know when their death will occur, sometimes right down to the day or hour. Surprisingly, they often face this knowledge not with fear or panic, but rather with quiet resignation. Their attempts to share information about the time of death may be very clear and direct. On the other hand, some may be so vague and subtle that others miss or ignore them, or label such messages "confused."

DOUG

Doug was in his late twenties. A born athlete who'd grown up in a family of sports fans, he'd played football in high school and college, then returned to his hometown as assistant football coach at his old high school.

He'd had his coaching job for a little more than two years when an enlarged lymph node in his neck was diagnosed as lymphoma. He tolerated six months of chemotherapy treatment so well he rarely missed any time at work. But the cancer returned, this time in many parts of his body, and attempts at treatment failed.

Unable to care for himself, Doug moved back in with his parents. He was referred to the local hospice program. We managed to get his symptoms under control; he was very weak, but was feeling fairly well and looked as if he would live for several months.

Doug's three siblings lived in the area and visited regularly. His parents provided most of his care, but the situation became strained when his youngest sister, Jane, was diagnosed as having cancer, too. Her chances for a cure were good, but the family decided not to tell Doug about her illness, for fear of upsetting him.

One Saturday evening Doug's father called the hospice. "Something seems different," he said.

When those of us who work with dying people hear that sentence we have learned to pay close attention. Sometimes patients or their families sense something is changing, but they can't describe it exactly. Responding to such a call we often find subtle but significant changes; sometimes the person actually is dying.

This time I arrived, talked with Doug and examined him, and could find no changes. Neither Doug nor his parents could say what was "different"—only that something was. I called the doctor anyway. She talked with Doug and suggested that she could come to the house or meet Doug at the hospital. Or we could wait and see if anything developed. Doug chose the last option. He and his parents were comfortable going to bed, knowing they could call me if necessary. Doug wanted to sleep. His parents said goodnight to him and offered me a cup of tea. We sat in the kitchen. I asked when Doug would be seeing his brother and sisters again.

"They'll all be over tomorrow afternoon to have dinner and watch the football game with us," his mother said. "This family is football crazy! Look at what Doug was doing today."

She handed me a piece of paper on which Doug had drawn a diagram of a football play, with circles and arrows indicating two teams and the directions to be taken by each player.

On one team, the six circles representing the players bore his initials and those of his parents and siblings. From the circle with Jane's initials an arrow ran to the edge of the field, but not out of bounds. The circle that bore Doug's initials had an arrow that went across the line and out of bounds: beside it he had scribbled, "Out of the game by noon on Sunday."

I studied the diagram.

"This might sound a little strange, but there may be something here that we ought to pay attention to," I said. "He seems to be saying that something serious might happen before noon tomorrow."

"What do you mean, 'something serious'?" his mother asked.

"I really don't know," I said. "But it could mean a change in his condition, or even that he might die."

At first skeptical, Doug's parents grew concerned.

"How about asking Doug to explain the diagram?" I asked. "He could probably explain this better than I."

"I don't want to wake him," his mother said. "We know Doug is ready to die. If that's what it means, I think we're prepared, and we can always call you again if something changes. I'll get hold of the other kids tomorrow and ask them to get here early."

In the morning, Doug was quieter than usual, but otherwise fine. Everyone arrived; each family member spent time with him. Just before noon Doug was lying in bed, talking with his mother. He suddenly became restless, saying he wasn't comfortable, then sat up and asked his mother to rearrange his pillows. He seemed to be having trouble breathing. Then he lay back, closed his eyes, and died.

"See how peaceful he looks?" his mother asked when I arrived to confirm his death. "He knew this was going to happen, didn't he?"

Doug hadn't died as a direct result of his cancer; curious about the sudden change, the doctor asked permission to do an autopsy and found that a fatal blood clot had traveled to Doug's lungs—a condition Doug couldn't have predicted.

"Maybe when you're close to dying you know more about death than anyone else," his father said. "I'm so glad he told us with that diagram."

Did Doug's drawing have any significance? Did he sense the time of his death, then use language familiar to his family to get that point across? Did he somehow know about Jane's illness, even though his family had withheld this information? Perhaps.

His drawing was symbolic, and consistent with one of his—and his family's—passions. It could have easily been missed. If we look, we can often find meaning in the communication of a dying person—even a scribbled football play. Understanding what he might have been saying helped Doug's family be a little more prepared for his death.

POLLY

A widow for nearly twenty years, Polly lived with her daughter, Sue. Ten years earlier she'd had a cancerous breast removed. For more than seven years she was apparently cancer free. But the disease returned, spreading to the bones and growing through the scar on her chest, causing an open wound with a foul-smelling discharge. Sometimes it would bleed—not dangerously, but enough to scare both mother and daughter. Polly's other main problem was pain, a common problem when cancer spreads to the bones.

Polly was physically and emotionally weary, tired of pain and of dressings that smelled bad or were soaked in blood. Sue was frustrated and worried. Her doctor had warned Sue that her mother's pain pills were very strong, so she gave them to Polly only when she thought her mother really needed them, fearing that frequent use would blunt their effectiveness.

Sue hated to change the dressing—it upset her mother to see it, and when she removed the dressing the wound often bled—so she delayed changing it as long as possible, which caused it to smell. No matter what she did, Sue felt she couldn't relieve her mother's suffering. She also worried that her two small daughters weren't receiving enough attention.

Because of Polly's extreme pain, the hospice program accepted her, even though her cancer wasn't immediately life threatening, to provide a month of home visits to see if we could ease her discomfort. The plan was to bring Polly's symptoms under control and boost Sue's skills and confidence in herself as a caregiver. By all accounts Polly would live quite a while; at the end of the month we planned to discharge her back to her own doctor's care.

During my first visit, Sue wept as she described her mother's pain; a tearless but exhausted Polly explained how discouraged she felt, and how she worried about her daughter.

"She spends so much time taking care of me she never has any time for her husband and little girls," Polly said. "It makes me feel so bad."

Within a week Polly's pain was under control. She and Sue better understood the use of pain-relieving medicines, and how even if a person develops a tolerance to them, the dosage can be increased safely to relieve pain. Sue was learning to manage her mother's care more effectively and efficiently; we showed her a simple way to clean and dress the chest wound that eliminated odors, stopped the bleeding, and needed to be done only once a day.

As Polly started to feel more comfortable, she took renewed interest in her granddaughters, and even volunteered to help with the housework. Halfway through the month of hospice care Polly, Sue, and I agreed they now needed only one visit a week.

I had a vacation scheduled; another nurse was to fill in for me. Just before the trip I said good-bye and reminded Sue and Polly that I'd see them in two weeks.

"But I won't be here," Polly said.

"What do you mean, Polly?" I asked.

"I'm not sure," she said. "I just have a feeling . . ."

Polly couldn't say more. Looking very doubtful, Sue asked what I thought. I said that although her mother was expected to live much longer she probably knew better than anyone, and asked Polly what she'd like to do. After some discussion Polly said she wanted everything to go on the way it was; however, she did want to see her sister and sole surviving sibling, Jeannie, with whom she'd had a less than perfect relationship.

As soon as Sue called, Jeannie traveled from another state to spend a few days. She and Polly had a wonderful visit—"the best time we've spent together in years," Jeannie told Sue as she was leaving for the airport.

The next week, Polly died in her sleep.

A few weeks later, Sue said, "I thought she had months and months to live. I'd have paid no attention to what Mother said if you hadn't told us it could be important. My aunt was a little annoyed when she arrived; here she was, rushing to catch a flight and interrupting her life and her sister looked so well. But after Mother died, Aunt Jeannie couldn't thank me enough for asking her to come.

"Those last two weeks were pretty amazing. I really didn't believe Mother would die so soon, and I wasn't worried, but I did find myself being much more affectionate with her. I didn't usually go around hugging and kissing Mother and telling her I loved her. But that week we had some very good talks. I told her how much I'd admired her courage when Dad died, and her strength when her cancer came back. And she told me I was her favorite child—I'm her only child!—and a pretty good nurse. She said I'd done a good job of caring for her.

"The night before Mother died I sat with her," Sue went on. "We talked—not about anything special, just little things. But it was nice and cozy. The next morning when I went into her room she was dead. She looked so peaceful, as if she'd just gone to sleep.

"The most amazing thing is that Mother knew she was dying and wasn't afraid. She didn't believe in God, or Heaven, or anything like that; once she said she didn't like the idea of disappearing into nothing. But she obviously knew she was going to be dying soon and she wasn't afraid, so I guess she thought it wouldn't be so bad. Most of all I'm glad she told us it would happen soon. I wouldn't have called Aunt Jeannie or said all I wanted to say, and I'd have missed the really special time we had."

This is the value of listening and believing when people tell us when they will die. If we hear the message we can use the time left to say and do things we want and need to do. We can say, "I love you," or "I'm so glad you were my friend," or "You have meant so much to me," or "I'm sorry for . . ." or even "I forgive you for . . ." Or, like Aunt Jeannie, we may see the person and have "the best visit in ages." If not given a warning, or if we don't hear it, we may find after a person dies that we regret not having taken the opportunity to say these things.

MICHAEL

Born with muscular dystrophy, Michael found even the smallest activities to be real challenges. But he was a determined young man, bright and creative, with a sunny disposition.

"My body doesn't cooperate with me, so I depend more on my mind," he said.

His illness and weakened condition left Michael prone to infections. Even a simple cold could develop easily into pneumonia; consequently, he was no stranger at the local hospital, where the doctors and nurses all knew and admired him. As he got older and more disabled, the infections became more frequent. The doctors were increasingly concerned about his dwindling strength and weakened lungs; they explained that any serious infection could be fatal. None of this daunted Michael, who still planned on going to college.

Because of his many hospitalizations, Michael was nearly twenty when he graduated from high school—with honors, as class valedictorian. He was thrilled when the state university accepted him; despite his parents' concern, he persuaded them that he could live on campus—"like a normal kid!"

They agreed to let him try. Wheelchair-bound, Michael needed help showering and dressing. To prevent his lungs from becoming congested, his position in bed had to be changed twice a night—something he couldn't do without help.

"Don't worry, I'm a Rambo on wheels!" he told his parents. "I'll figure it out."

Michael soon formed a loyal group of campus friends who took turns helping him; dorm neighbors set their alarm clocks so they could help him change position during the night. The nurses in the student health clinic also kept a close eye on Michael, urging him to stay in the clinic whenever necessary. His buddies would camp out with him in the clinic to "make sure those nurses were taking care of him right." Laughter followed this crowd wherever they went, and the nurses never objected to "Michael's pajama parties."

He survived his first year of college with only minor setbacks. But in his second year a flu epidemic spread across campus and Michael became ill. He developed pneumonia and was immediately sent to the hospital. So many times before Michael had been very ill but had recovered. Although his friends were also very concerned, Michael once again seemed to be responding to the antibiotic treatments. They all breathed sighs of relief and returned to their daily routines. The next day his father received a puzzling phone call at work.

"I love you, Dad," Michael said. "And I want to thank you for being such a good father."

"Michael, I'll see you this evening when I get off work," his father said.

"Oh, Dad, I won't be able to tell you then," he answered.

Remembering the crowd of young people that always seemed to fill Michael's room, his father assumed he was referring to the lack of privacy.

"I love you too, Mikey. You're a good kid and I'll see you later,' his father said, not knowing that all afternoon Michael had been placing similar calls to his mother, brother, and friends. When they all arrived at the hospital that evening, he was in a coma from which he never awoke. Michael died that night with the people he loved around him.

Caring for a dying person is hard work, especially at home. There are medications to be given, often around the clock, personal care to be done, meals to prepare, and sometimes dressings or treatments to do. And despite all of this, the tide of usual day-to-day responsibilities continues: bills must be paid, children must be cared for, laundry must be done. Families are frequently tired and it's a massive job merely to focus on a particular day or a given moment. The future holds grief and loss, so many families and friends avoid looking ahead.

Michael's family easily missed the information they were given. Polly's daughter wouldn't have believed her mother's message, had it not been explained. Both messages clearly indicated an awareness of the future that families often subconsciously deny—not because they don't care or aren't interested, but because they don't understand the significance of what's being said. Busy providing care and emotional support, they can't see beyond these immediate concerns.

If such direct communication can be missed or misinterpreted, it's easy to see how subtle messages can be overlooked or misconstrued.

ILSA

"Mother wouldn't think of meeting you without being dressed and having her makeup on," Betty explained as she greeted me. "I hope you don't mind waiting. She gave me specific instructions to entertain you while the nurse's aide helps her get ready. Come into the breakfast room and we'll have a cup of tea."

It was a bright August morning as we sat in front of the lovely sun-filled bay window. I asked Betty to tell me more about her mother. She smiled.

"My mother may look small and frail, but she's always been independent, with a strong sense of values. She and my father left Germany just before World War II broke out, without much more than a few possessions and the clothes on their backs. I was born here. It took a lot of hard work to reestablish themselves, but they did, and my father built a successful business. He died when I was six, so I was really raised by my mother. She managed the company until she retired last year—and only then because she was sick.

"When she was diagnosed with colon cancer, we asked her

to come and live with us, but she refused—not wanting to be a burden on us, or leave her home and friends in Philadelphia. Last month she called and said she'd changed her mind. Her friends tell me that what really got her to come here was a series of falls that frightened her. She still hasn't mentioned them to me. She's very stoic. I feel sad because I know it was hard for her to leave Philly, even though she never talks about it, but I'm so relieved to have her here. We were very worried about her living alone."

I asked Betty how she'd been managing her mother's care.

"She's insisted on hiring her own nurse's aide, so I won't have to take care of her personal needs. This bothered me at first because I wouldn't have considered it a burden. I don't work and the kids are in school, but my husband and I decided to go along with her wishes since it seemed so important to her that she make her own decisions."

I agreed that was probably the best plan as it allowed her mother to maintain some control.

Suddenly we heard the ringing of a porcelain bell.

"Mother's ready for you!" Betty said with a smile. She escorted me into the library, where Ilsa sat regally in a chair by the fireplace.

"I'm sorry to have kept you waiting," she said in a charming German accent as we shook hands. "This illness has slowed me down a bit. But perhaps you've had a chance to get to know my daughter. Isn't she wonderful? She and her family just moved into this lovely home a year ago, and she's done all the decorating by herself!

"Betty! Did you show her the Christmas wreaths you've been making?" Ilsa asked. "I was born in Germany, the country where so many Christmas traditions started, so we're already preparing for the holiday, even though it's months away! Christmas has always been the most important day in the year for our family. It's such a happy time."

Each week I visited, Ilsa would direct Betty to show me their latest Christmas project.

"I know this will be her last Christmas, so we're trying to

make this the best one she's ever had," Betty said sadly to me. "But I keep pushing it out of my mind. She's always been in the middle of all the festivities. It's hard to imagine Christmas without her."

By October Ilsa had grown far weaker and was spending more time in bed. She rarely complained but no longer seemed interested in helping with the decorations. Betty reported that she had become quiet and withdrawn, and appeared depressed.

"I keep trying to do more and more to perk her up and make her feel better, and it only seems to make her more withdrawn," she said.

Depression is a normal part of dealing with the many losses experienced in the process of dying. And as with other emotions, depression should be respected. When I told Betty this, she seemed relieved. I suggested that she spend time just sitting quietly with her mother.

"The other day she said that Christmas can be a sad time, too. Perhaps she realizes this will be her last Christmas with us," Betty said sadly.

"Yes, that could be it," I replied. "But it could also mean that your mother might be aware that she could die sometime during the holidays."

Betty was surprised and a little shaken by this thought.

"It's really too early to tell," I said. "Just keep doing what you're already doing so well—making each day the best it can be for her."

Ilsa became weaker as the holidays approached. Although her care was going well at Betty's house, she asked to be admitted to the hospice inpatient unit to die. Betty really wanted her mother to stay at home but, again respecting her mother's wishes, she agreed. Ilsa was admitted to the unit on December 20.

Betty and her family spent Christmas Eve visiting with Ilsa, enjoying the carolers and festive atmosphere. As they were preparing to leave, Ilsa whispered instructions to her daughter for finding the gifts that had been hidden around the house. Betty was touched to learn that the nurse's aide had secretly shopped for her mother and helped her wrap and hide the gifts back in October. Betty kissed Ilsa and everyone wished her a merry Christmas as they headed for home.

The next morning, after opening all their gifts, they were preparing to leave for the hospice unit. The phone rang. Ilsa had just died—peacefully, without any warning.

I visited Betty the next day. She tearfully told me her ten-year-old had said, "Now Christmas will always be Grandma's day, so you see, Mom, she will always be right here with us!"

"I'm glad Mother warned me in October," Betty said. "I had all that time to think of it in a different way. Otherwise it would have been devastating to have her die on that day. She must have known somehow, and wanted to prepare me."

Ilsa's clear but subtle comment—about the possible timing of her death—didn't change anything, but it did allow time for her daughter and family to prepare for that possibility. By living with this thought, they were able to become more comfortable with it and look at it in a different, more positive way than if it had come as a surprise.

NICHOLAS

"I live the American dream," Nicholas said when I first met him. "I'm a man who had everything until this damn cancer hit—a good marriage, three successful children, a big house, and the best Greek restaurant in the city. My employees aren't just employees, they're members of my family."

The son of poor Greek immigrants, Nick was indeed successful, well respected, and loved by many. Scores of friends helped with his care after he became ill with stomach cancer at fifty-five. But the illness took a mean turn when Nick couldn't eat anymore without getting sick to his stomach.

"It's ironic," he said. "I'm not hungry at all, it's just that I really miss the pleasure of food. It's been my life!"

"Every day he calls the cook at the restaurant to bring him something different for dinner," his wife Christina said. "And every day the cook rushes over with exactly what Nick wants. Everyone knows he can't eat it, but he orders it anyway!"

In early June Christina called, concerned about the way Nick was acting.

"Maybe you'd better come over and check him," she said. "I think he's getting confused."

When I arrived, he was busy directing his wife to "get the sparkler cake now."

"See? He's all confused," Christina said. "Our wedding anniversary is the Fourth of July, so the cook always makes us a big cake with sparklers on it—but that's more than a month away. I keep trying to explain this to Nick, but he keeps asking for the cake."

I examined Nick carefully but could find no physical reason for this sudden change. I suggested to Christina that Nick might be more aware of what was happening to him than we were. Perhaps he was trying to tell her that he would die before their anniversary.

Upset, Christina called the family together to discuss this, and they agreed to get the cake and have the celebration the next day. It was a great party and Nick was unusually bright and active. To everyone's amazement, he even managed to eat a small piece of cake without getting sick.

Nick died on June 30 and was buried on July 4, his wedding anniversary. At the cemetery Christina hugged me.

"Let me tell you what Nick said to me during the party," she said in tears. "He told me he was proud of me as a woman, and as a wife, and he was proud of the twenty-six happy years we've had together. He thanked me and I cried and cried. But I thanked him, too. I'm so glad we celebrated our anniversary early. But we almost missed having that wonderful day because I thought he was just confused."

. . .

In subtle and indirect ways, both Ilsa and Nicholas shared their special knowledge of when death would occur with the people they loved. Ilsa was clear; Nicholas's family thought he was confused. Either message easily could have been missed.

Why don't dying people simply say, "I'm dying on this particular day or at this exact time"?

We don't know. There is much we have yet to learn and understand about Nearing Death Awareness. But, in ways that are direct, or subtle, or even silent, dying people *are* showing us that they *do* know when their deaths will occur, and that they are not distressed by this information. By listening and understanding these messages, we are given unique opportunities to prepare ourselves for their loss, to deal with our fears of dying, to use well the time that is left, and to participate more significantly in this life event.

III

NEARING
DEATH
AWARENESS:
WHAT
I NEED
FOR A
PEACEFUL
DEATH

.

THIS section of the book covers requests for what a person needs to die peacefully. Some people realize a need for reconciliation. Some request the removal of a barrier standing in the way of a peaceful death. Still others need particular circumstances to die peacefully—perhaps choosing the time of their death or the people who will be there.

Realizing what they need, dying people often become concerned; some communicate a tremendous urgency. Coherent requests usually bring action. But requests that are vague or indirect may be missed or ignored, leading to frustration, anxiety, and sometimes agitation. If the awareness of an important need comes late—when death seems to be imminent—the person may delay or prolong the process of dying in an attempt to settle an issue or effect a final reconciliatory meeting.

A person's anxiety, agitation, or prolonged dying can be upsetting for everyone—patient, family members and friends, and health-care workers. Often, the response to agitation is to sedate the patient—and sometimes the family. Sedatives may help relieve agitation, but medicines alone are not the answer. Trying to stifle agitation without analyzing it and, if possible, attempting to bring about a resolution of the underlying matter, may increase rather than decrease the distress.

Understanding issues that need resolution can enable us to better assist dying people and help us realize the need for reconciliation and completion in our own lives.

CHAPTER TEN

"WE *MUST* GO TO THE PARK."

ANDREA

Walking through the front door of Andrea's comfortable suburban home, I introduced myself.

"I have some questions to ask you," she said in a businesslike manner.

Her husband, Tom, stood behind her with a look of calm curiosity, holding the youngest of their three little children; the other two were sprawled out on the kitchen floor, busy with their coloring books.

"I need to know who you are," Andrea said to me as she put on a coffeepot. We sat together at the kitchen table as I briefly told her about my professional background.

"Why do you do this work?" she asked in the same direct, efficient manner. "Isn't it depressing?"

"That's a hard question to answer," I said. "The sadness and tragedy of somebody's dying is always there—I feel it, too. But beyond that is an opportunity for me to help a patient cherish the final chapter of her life, to use this time to resolve issues, say important things, finish unfinished business, and share important moments with people she cares about.

"My job is to keep my patients as comfortable as possible—not just physically—so they can do those things and use this special time the best way they can. I also feel strongly that, like birthing, dying can be an opportunity for the whole family to share positive experiences, rather than only sadness, pain, and loss. That is the challenge of this work, and that's the joy for me."

Andrea was quiet for a few minutes, then smiled and poured me another cup of coffee. I realized that I hadn't finished my "job interview" yet.

"I have uterine cancer, and have been told I'm dying," she said. "I want to know what it's going to be like."

I was amazed at the lack of fear in the eyes of this remarkable twenty-nine-year-old woman. And clearly it was not unusual for this couple to talk so openly with their young children present.

"I have never died," I said, "so I can't tell you from personal experience. But I have cared for dying people for many years now, so I can tell you what I've seen and what they've told me."

"Great!" she said. "I'd like to hear about that!"

I started by telling her of the physical changes that were common with her disease: loss of appetite, with resulting weight loss, weakness, some pain, and possibly some mild nausea.

I explained how we would try to control the various discomforts she might develop, using diet changes and medications. I explained she probably would experience increasing sleepiness and dreaminess—perhaps some confusion toward the end— leading to a brief coma before she died. She probably would die of liver failure, but with proper symptom control we would be able to keep her comfortable.

"Okay, that's what's going to happen to my body," she said. "But what's going to happen to *me?*"

She was curious and amazed when I told her about Nearing Death Awareness—that other patients had talked of being with someone who had died already, getting ready to leave, seeing where they were going, and knowing when it would happen. I told her they also showed us they were not powerless in this process, and were often able to tell us what they needed to die peacefully, and even choose the actual time they died.

I assured Andrea that in all my experience, with rare exception, I hadn't seen painful or frightening deaths. She seemed surprised and relieved.

I gave Andrea a copy of Dr. Raymond Moody's book, *Life After Life*, which describes near-death experiences, suggesting that she might get additional information from it.

I explained that although she *might* have near-death experiences, as she got closer to dying her experiences probably would be different from these, possibly much slower and more gradual, and she might be able to share them with the people around her as they actually happened. She was very excited about this.

The conversation had taken two hours and the day was quickly disappearing.

"I was *supposed* to tell you about the hospice program and how it could be of help to you!" I said. We laughed.

"You've told me what I really needed to know," she said. "When will you come back?"

On my next visit, Andrea greeted me at the door; she was excited.

"Tom and I read the book together," she said. "It was *so* helpful; we read parts of it to the kids. If that's what dying is like, I think I can do it!"

I was touched by her remark—"I think I can do it!" Not "I want to," but "If I have to, I think I can!" This information clearly helped Andrea feel less frightened and powerless about dying.

"I'm fascinated," she said. "This information has really helped me. So I want to help you any way I can, so you can help others. I tell you what, if any of these things happen to me, I *promise* to tell you all about it. Okay?" So we had a pact early in our relationship.

Being involved with Andrea, Tom, and their young children was a delight. Their openness, desire for honesty, and ability to work out difficulties as a family amazed me. I applauded them for involving the children in all that was done or discussed, as I knew it would play a major role in how well they would deal with this tragedy now, and the process of grieving later.

"We've always included them," Andrea said. "We believe honesty is the best policy with kids. But, even if we didn't, how could we have a private conversation with three kids under the age of seven underfoot?" She laughed.

I asked how the kids had reacted to the book.

"They thought it was neat," Andrea said. "Lisa said it sounded like magic!"

One day I arrived to find Andrea in tears, silently sitting on the living-room floor, surrounded by three grocery bags—one for each child.

"These are the kids' baby books," she said. "I never had time to put them together properly."

"Look at my beautiful babies!" she said, handing me some pictures. "How I *hate* having to leave them! I'm afraid they'll forget me, so I want each one to have something special to remember me by. Would you help me? It's too hard for Tom to do."

I sat on the floor with her. Together we cried, shared the tissues, and started working on three little books, each titled "Mommy and Me." I felt drained by sadness but filled with admiration for this beautiful young mother.

Three weeks later, I happened to be driving through Andrea's neighborhood. Her routine visit wasn't scheduled, but my day had ended early; having some extra time I decided to stop by. Andrea met me at the door, looking very pale but pleased to see me.

"What a surprise!" she said. "I was just thinking about you. Come on in!"

She started to sway as if dizzy.

"I'm going to be sick," she mumbled.

I grabbed her arm as she stumbled past me to the bathroom. I shouted for Tom to come quickly as Andrea fainted in my arms. Awkwardly we lowered her to the floor. She was hemorrhaging.

Tom was panic-stricken.

"Don't tell me this is it!" he said. "Isn't there anything we can do?"

"They may be able to reverse this with aggressive treatment in the hospital," I said. "Or we can keep her comfortable here at home. But if she loses too much blood, she'll die very soon.

Andrea said she didn't want any more treatment for the cancer, but what do you think she'd want us to do in this situation?"

"It's too sudden!" he said. "She's not ready yet—and neither are we." He started sobbing. "There are things she wants to finish for the kids. And she'd just started helping me figure out the family finances. If it's possible to buy a little more time—I think we need it—she'd want us to try."

We called the ambulance. Andrea was admitted to the hospital Intensive Care Unit, where she responded to treatments and blood transfusions, finally regaining consciousness. I was allowed in to see her.

"Andrea, I'm so glad you're feeling better," I said. "We all had quite a scare!"

She reached for my hand and held it very tightly.

Remembering the look on her face before she became unconscious, I suspected Andrea had experiences we couldn't see, and felt sure she'd share those with me if she could.

"Did anything happen?" I asked. I could see her struggle to put her thoughts into words. It's impossible to describe the look in her eyes as she stared intently at me. Awe? Wonder? Amazement?

"Did something good happen?" I asked.

"Yes," she murmured. "Oh yes!"

"Can you tell me anything about it—even just a word?" I asked.

"I can't," she whispered. "I just can't!" She slowly shook her head.

"Don't worry," I said. "It's okay—maybe later. I'm just so glad you're back and it was a good experience for you."

Andrea never was able to describe what happened to her that day, but there was a peace and tranquility about her that was felt by all around her.

"Andrea puts on a brave front to protect others from her pain and fears," Tom said a few weeks later. "That's her way of making it easy for them. Every now and then she'll let me hold her and we cry about what's happening to us, but not too often.

"She won't say anything, but I know she's hurt about the way my father has acted," he continued. "The two of them

became pretty close after her parents died. I think she and Pop
really love each other. He's not much of a talker, but they got
along great, anyway.

"After he retired and my mother died, he'd come by every
day to help Andrea with the kids. But that was *before* she got
sick.

"When we told him about her cancer, he flew into a rage,
shouting at both of us. We were speechless and it really upset
the children."

" 'Give him time,' Andrea told me. 'He needs to work this
out on his own. He's just too upset right now.' " There was an
angry edge in Tom's voice.

"Well, time turned into weeks and things didn't get better,"
he said. "Pop stopped by occasionally, but didn't stay long and
was gruff and abrupt. I came home from work after one of his
visits and found Andrea in tears. 'I feel like he's angry at *me*
because I might die and leave you stuck to raise these kids alone,'
she sobbed. 'Does he think I would *choose* this to happen?'

"Let me tell you," Tom said, "I could've killed him on the
spot! I grabbed that phone so fast and called him. 'Damn it,' I
shouted, 'we've got enough going on without putting up with
you, too!'—and slammed the phone down. We haven't seen him
since. It's so unlike him. How can he be so cruel?"

Judging from the description of Pop's behavior before Andrea's
diagnosis, I suggested that perhaps his father actually loved
Andrea so much he couldn't deal with losing her—or face the
changes that were happening.

"You and Andrea have met our social worker," I said. "I feel
certain he could help with this problem. I truly think Pop's
suffering a lot of emotional pain himself right now."

"You're right!" Tom said. "The social worker has been real
helpful. Maybe he could talk to Pop. I'd rather not deal with
him myself."

Our social worker visited Pop and reported that he was so
devastated about Andrea's illness that he was overwhelmed by
rage, grief, and fear. "How can something like this happen?"
he'd said. "I don't know what to say! I don't know what to do!
Andrea acts so brave. I'm afraid I'll lose control and break down

every time I look at her. I love her so much; she's the daughter I never had. Then I look at those babies and I just can't bear it—she's such a good mother—what will become of them? How can Tom possibly manage all this and support his family, too?"

The social worker visited regularly and was able to help Pop begin to recognize his feelings and confront his fears. But we all felt a sense of urgency for this reconciliation to take place, as Andrea was now deteriorating rapidly.

She'd been able to finish the financial work she'd started with Tom and the books she lovingly made for each of her children. She had hired a woman to care for the kids while Tom was working. And as though knowing that her work was done, she seemed to just "let go."

Andrea was in bed all the time now, so I suggested a hospital bed might be easier.

"We don't want one," Tom said. "There won't be room for me and the kids in a hospital bed!"

Too weak to participate in any of her care, Andrea slept most of the time and had increasing periods of restlessness and confusion. But a clear and insistent phrase in her incoherent ramblings was "We *must* go to the park." I asked Tom what that might mean. I was concerned that her restlessness indicated that something was making her uncomfortable.

"She and Pop used to take the kids to the park all the time," he said. "It's Pop she's waiting for—I'm certain! She's suffered long enough; I'm going to get him and bring him here right now, whether he's ready to come now or not!"

Eyes blurred with tears, Pop could barely navigate the stairs of his son's home. When he saw Andrea, he exploded into sobs, cradling her in his arms.

"I'm here, sweetheart, I'm here," he said. "I'm so sorry. Please forgive me. I love you so much! I'll never stay away again. I'll come every day. I promise!" Andrea's eyelids fluttered as she barely whispered, "Pop."

"Could I stay here tonight?" Pop asked.

"Yes, we'd like that," Tom said.

Andrea died peacefully that evening, in their king-sized bed, surrounded by Tom, her children, and Pop.

Moments after I arrived, Tom told me that, as Andrea was dying, their daughter Lisa—who must have remembered the descriptions of leaving the body as part of Near Death Experiences described in the book they'd read—looked up to the ceiling and, waving, called out, "Bye, Mom. We love you! Have a good magic trip and don't forget to save us front-row seats in Heaven!"

CHAPTER ELEVEN

NEEDING RECONCILIATION: "I NEED TO MAKE PEACE WITH..."

One of the most important aspects of Nearing Death Awareness is the need for reconciliation. Dying people develop an awareness that they need to be at peace. As death nears, people often realize some things feel unfinished or incomplete—perhaps issues that once seemed insignificant or that happened long ago. Now the dying person realizes their importance and wants to settle them. If this awareness comes late—when death seems imminent—the person may delay or prolong dying in an attempt to effect a reconciliatory meeting, as in the previous story when Andrea waited for her father-in-law.

If a request for reconciliation is made coherently, most people try to help. For example, if a dying man says: "I need to speak to my sister. We haven't spoken since we had a horrible argument fifteen years ago," most people do what they can to try to find his sister.

But sometimes the request is less clear. It may be missed, seen as unimportant, or labeled as confusion. If dying people know what needs to be reconciled, but their attempts to communicate their needs are ignored, they may become agitated. This often happens if they are close to death and realize death won't be peaceful without this reconciliation. This may be what occurs when someone seems to die in pain; rather than physical, the pain may be emotional or spiritual. These types of pain can be harder to relieve, and far too often go unidentified or ignored.

The underlying issues tend to revolve around relationships—hence the strong drive in many dying people to search for healing and reconciliation, whether with other people, with a supreme being, or with themselves.

THERESA

Theresa, twenty-two, was dying of bone cancer. She was the younger of two children, abandoned by their father when she was five. Though he lived nearby, the father had had little contact with his son and daughter over the years, and had contributed nothing toward their upbringing. Theresa lived with her mother, who took care of her; her brother, who lived nearby, visited frequently and did what he could to help.

During my first visit, Theresa and her mother described the father as "that man," not "my father," or "my ex-husband." I asked if Theresa wanted to see him. She said that since they had no relationship she didn't feel any need to do so.

Theresa's biggest problems were pain and weight loss. As often happens with young people, whose metabolisms run faster than those of older people, Theresa's pain required fairly large doses of pain medicine. We tried other pain-relieving techniques also: Theresa found meditation and music particularly helpful, and we instituted a regular schedule for those.

The weight loss was difficult for her mother to see. Theresa was five feet seven, and had always been slim. But now she ate very little and refused all dietary supplements. As she became weaker and spent more time in bed, her mother had to turn her from side to side every few hours to prevent bedsores.

Four months after admission into our program Theresa was dying. Her pain became increasingly severe; the dosage of her pain medicines had risen accordingly. We thought her physical pain was controlled, but still she moaned. We asked what the matter was, but couldn't get an answer; her speech was difficult to understand. Several times her mother asked me how Theresa could still be alive.

But one day, mixed in among a jumble of words, she said, "Dad."

We wondered if she wanted to see her father. We asked her, but her response was unintelligible, a few words lost in another moan. Her mother felt it was worth a try. She telephoned the father and explained what was happening.

That afternoon Theresa's brother picked up the father and brought him to the apartment.

He went into the bedroom, sat beside Theresa, held her hand, and told her he was there. He said no more. He looked shaken and upset, but also stiff and uncomfortable. After a few minutes he stood.

"I can't take this," he said, leaving the room and saying an awkward farewell.

But Theresa's moaning stopped, her agitation eased, and she died quietly a few hours later. No one can say that her estranged father's visit was what Theresa needed for a peaceful death. But the only circumstance making that day different from those preceding it was his presence. Her mother and brother feel that in some way Theresa needed something from her father, and that after his visit she was able to let go and die.

Theresa realized very late that she needed to see her father; her weakened condition kept her from being able to communicate intelligibly. Any delay in getting her father to come arose from our difficulty in understanding her; finding and bringing her father to see her was easy. Sometimes it can be hard to find the important person, which can lead to much frustration.

SHEILA

In a thick brogue Sheila's nephew described her background during my first visit.

"She had great promise," he said. "But with so little in the way of opportunity for such a girl in the old country, her family pooled their meager resources and sent her to America. The poor little thing was an innocent wisp of a girl. Traveling alone at eighteen, she sailed to this country in steerage: they were packed in like animals. It's a wonder she survived the trip."

Like so many Irish girls of her generation, Sheila immigrated to America, worked as a maid, sent money home, and lived a lonely life—until she met a boy and fell in love. The love didn't last, but the daughter born of it did, and Sheila found herself out on the street, struggling to keep herself and her infant daughter, Maureen, alive.

"Those were hard days," the nephew said. "Until Sheila met Mr. O'Malley, a farmer. He's years older, but a hard-working man, and has provided well for her all these years. He's never had any use for Maureen, though, because she's illegitimate. He sent her to boarding school when she was seven, and allowed her home to visit only twice a year."

"Where is Maureen now?" I asked.

"Maureen turned out to be a good-for-nothing, and no one knows her whereabouts," he said. "It's like a knife in poor Sheila's heart, but she never mentions her name. It's like she's dead!"

Despite their fifty-five-year marriage, Sheila always referred to her husband as "Mr. O'Malley" or "himself." He was a man of few words and gruff by nature, but surprisingly active and strong for a man in his eighties, doing the daily chores around their farm. Their relationship did not seem to be a warm and affectionate one, but rather one of quiet dependency, or perhaps comfortable tolerance. What care Mr. O'Malley was unable to give Sheila was provided by the live-in help he'd hired.

Sheila was dying at home of uterine cancer. As her condition deteriorated, she became more and more depressed and quiet—often refusing to eat, instead just staring off into space sadly.

"I want this to be done," she'd say, but lingered on as if waiting for something.

"Sheila, it seems like you're waiting for something," I said. "Is it Maureen?"

Sheila's eyes filled with tears. She waved her hand as though pushing the conversation away, rolled onto her side, and closed her eyes.

She battled one complication after another: in her weakened condition, she seemed likely to die with each problem. But she hung on, and the hospice team members discussed their sense that Sheila was waiting to see someone before she died—probably Maureen.

The chaplain, the social worker, and I visited one day, hoping that together we could discuss our concern with Mr. O'Malley. Was there some way to determine Maureen's whereabouts and notify her that her mother was dying and needed to see her?

"There'll be no such talk in this house!" Mr. O'Malley shouted, becoming irate. "That girl's been nothing but heartache and trouble since the day she was born. I won't hear of it!" he roared, waving his cane around as he stormed out the back door.

But within the week Sheila's cousin Eileen timidly called the chaplain to report that some months before Maureen had sent her a letter postmarked in Florida with her return address. In the letter Maureen asked how her mother was, explaining that she had written many times and never received an answer. She went on to say that she knew she had caused her mother great sorrow, but was now in an alcoholic-treatment program and was trying to pick up the pieces of her life. She wanted her mother to be given the message that she loved her and was sorry for having caused so much trouble.

Eileen knew Sheila relied on Mr. O'Malley to read the mail to her and suspected he had hidden Maureen's letters. She felt guilty for not giving Maureen's message to Sheila, but was afraid to deal with Mr. O'Malley's wrath. "He's a fierce man, that one!" she said.

Eileen told the chaplain about Maureen's harsh upbringing and of Sheila's timidity in the face of her husband's domineering personality. The last thread between Sheila and her daughter was broken when, after running away from school, Maureen became a hippie, and came home to ask for money. Her stepfather threw her out, threatening to call the police if she ever returned.

"Sheila's heart was broken," Eileen said, sadly. "She never saw Maureen again, nor did she mention her name. That was almost twenty years ago. We heard she'd married and had two children, but divorced and lost custody of them because of her drinking."

The next day, I went with the chaplain as he confronted Mr. O'Malley with this information. He became angry and defensive.

"It's a husband's job to protect his wife!" he stormed. In a gentle, kind way, the chaplain then explained to Sheila what had happened. She defiantly looked her husband straight in the eye.

"O'Malley, you're the devil himself!" she said. With that he threw a handful of letters on her bed and stormed out. They were all from Maureen. The chaplain read them as tears rolled down Sheila's thin cheeks.

"Bring her to me!" she pleaded.

Needing to maintain his lifetime pattern of control over others, Mr. O'Malley refused to pay for Maureen's airplane ticket, or allow her to sleep in his home, but other relatives chipped in for the ticket and provided her with a place to stay.

Sheila was too weak to get out of bed, sleeping most of the time, but on the day her daughter arrived, she was alert and bright with anticipation. Maureen indeed showed the signs of many years of self-abuse, but there wasn't a dry eye in the room when Maureen rushed into her mother's arms. They wept silently, holding each other for what seemed like hours. Mr. O'Malley spent the day in the barn with his animals.

Maureen spent as much time with her mother as Mr. O'Malley would permit; each day he seemed to allow a little more. She bathed her mother, massaged her feet with lotion, and gently brushed her long white hair. She sat for hours, patiently spoon-feeding the dying woman puddings and applesauce. It was a close and tender time for both of them.

Finally one day Mr. O'Malley announced, "You can stay here tonight if you wish." Maureen sat by her mother's bed all that night, humming the songs she remembered Sheila's singing to her when she was a small child. Sheila peacefully drifted off to sleep, quietly slipped into a coma, and died at dawn with Maureen holding her hand.

The hospice chaplain took up a collection so Maureen could buy a nice dress for her mother's funeral. Despite her sorrow, Maureen looked younger and healthier than she had when she arrived only three weeks before.

Another theme that recurs is reconciliation with a supreme being. Those who belong to a religious congregation often want the support, prayers, and blessings of that community as they prepare for death. But the same need may occur in people not committed to an organized religion, in those who disavow the spiritual, and in those who have lost whatever faith they once might have had.

ARTHUR

Arthur had had cancer for years, but had responded well to treatment. Now the cancer was active again and he was dying slowly in his small, neat apartment. He lived alone and had no relatives; his wife had died five years before. He had married her soon after his first wife left him—an event that began his drift away from the Episcopal faith in which he'd been raised. It had been decades since he'd set foot in a church.

"God and I have a good relationship," he'd say. "We don't need any go-between."

Arthur kept his condition to himself; he didn't want to burden his friends by asking for help, and resisted offers of assistance, from friends or professionals. He contacted the hospice because his doctor had suggested a nursing home, and the manager of his apartment building had explained how hospice helps to keep people at home. He was wary that we too would push him toward an institution, but once he knew us better, he was pleased to see any of the hospice staff.

"I like you people," he'd say. "You come and check on me, show me how to feel better, and then you go away and leave me alone!"

As he got sicker, we urged him to let us arrange for someone to be with him, especially at night. He refused until he became so weak that we thought it was no longer safe for him to be alone, and persuaded him to have a nurse stay at night.

By now Arthur had a partial bowel obstruction that caused pain, which we relieved with injections every few hours. He could tolerate little more than sips of water or dietary supplements, and often vomited. Even so, he insisted that he wanted to be at home, with as little attention as possible.

One afternoon the hospice doctor visited to check Arthur's condition. As she was getting ready to leave, he said, "Would you pray with me, please?"

The doctor held Arthur's hand and said a prayer, then asked if he needed anything else.

"Would it be too much trouble to have a priest come to see me?" Arthur asked.

"Of course not," she said. "Do you want to see one tonight?"

"No, not tonight," Arthur said. "Tomorrow would be fine."

The next morning I brought an Episcopal priest with me. A friendly man in his early thirties, he greeted Arthur warmly. I checked Arthur's vital signs, then left, telling him I'd complete my nursing visit later that day. When I returned he thanked me for bringing the clergyman by.

"He stayed for an hour or so, and I really enjoyed it," Arthur said. "I can't believe how much better I feel. We talked, he said the prayers of absolution, and he anointed me with oil. It's strange; nothing has really changed, but I feel much easier."

That evening the priest returned, bringing Arthur communion. Afterward they prayed together, then talked for a while, sipping whiskeys. Arthur died quietly in his sleep early the next morning.

His condition had led us to expect Arthur to die for more than two weeks. The day before he died, there were no significant physical changes; the only difference was his interaction with the clergyman. We think Arthur died that night because the priest had helped him become reconciled to a church with which he had once had strong ties.

Arthur's request was straightforward—he simply asked to see a priest. When the request is not as clear it may take onlookers longer to understand, and this can lead to great frustration or anguish for the one dying.

GUS

As strange as it may seem to others, those of us who work with dying people become accustomed to the physical changes that are so often distressing to see. The profound weight loss experienced by many dying people can be a very upsetting symptom for family and friends. But as we get to know these patients they become beautiful in our eyes, despite their frail and chiseled appearance.

My immediate reaction when Gus answered the door for my first visit was that I had the wrong apartment. Here was a tall, handsome, well-nourished man in his early fifties, certainly not thin or frail-looking. Except for the molded neck brace that held his head rigid, he looked healthy.

"How about a beer?" he said. "It's almost noon! I never drink before noon! But, damn, I don't get up until eleven-thirty!" He laughed heartily.

I was beginning to realize that Gus had a strong will and enjoyed being a tease. He especially delighted in using rough language.

Gus's cancer was dangerously near the spinal cord in his neck. Considering his medical report, I was amazed to see that he was so functional.

"I'm on sick leave from the precinct," Gus said. "The captain is pushing me to go on disability leave, but no way! I can still work. By the way, my ex-wife wants you to call her. She just lives two blocks away."

His ex-wife, Kim, asked to meet me at the local fast-food restaurant.

"I divorced Gus six years ago," she said. "I love the man, but I couldn't take it. He was crazy about being a Marine and just couldn't get enough combat. He requested assignment to Vietnam THREE times! Can you believe that? And I was left alone with the kids. While he was there, he was exposed to Agent Orange, and we suspect that's how he got the cancers.

"After his last tour, I had my little boy," she said, her eyes filling with tears. "He died from birth defects when he was only three months old. Gus dealt with that by partying and drinking more. He quit the Marines and joined the police, asking to work in the worst precinct in the city as an undercover cop. That was the last straw. I was just plain worn out—always living on the edge of danger and crisis. I had my kids to think about. But we live real close and the kids see him regularly.

"Then he got the cancer," she said. "The treatments were hard on him, but he's a tough guy and insisted on as much as he could possibly have done. The doctor says he's terminal now, but he won't believe it! I go over every day to check on him; I need to help him through this for the kids—they're too young to be losing their Dad. I guess I'm doing it a little bit for me, too. I do love him, I just can't live with him. I don't know how we're going to get through this. But however we do, it will be his way, I can tell you that!"

Gus continued to be his strong, independent, and colorful self for a few weeks, enjoying his beer and playing cards with his buddies. Then the cancer grew into his spinal cord and he quickly became paralyzed, bedridden, and confused. Private-duty nurses were put in to help Kim and his family take care of him. He was comfortable, but it was clear that he was dying quickly.

I received an urgent call from the nurse on duty.

"Please get out here fast," she said. "Everything seemed to be going okay but now he's very confused and anxious, and we're losing it."

"No, I bet we're finally getting it," I thought to myself. I had wondered how long Gus would be able to keep up the tough-guy façade. I felt there must be times he felt frightened—even if he wouldn't talk about it, or allow his fear to show.

The scene was chaotic. Gus was crying out in anguish; his speech was so disjointed it was hard to make any sense of it. But in his confused language were the words "villages," "babies," "napalm," "burning"—and the tragic words "I did it, I did it!" In the middle of this swirling jumble was the sentence "I need religious integrity!"

Gus had been clear on my first visit that he was raised in a churchgoing family, but religion had not been important to him in his adult life. However, he did enjoy a few visits from the hospice chaplain, so I called him.

"Can you come quickly?" I asked. "I think you are the one who can fix this."

Kim, the children, and Gus's parents and brothers were all there when the chaplain arrived. We sat together in the kitchen so the chaplain could talk with Gus privately. Minutes passed; and slowly the cries stopped. The house became peaceful. The chaplain called the family into the bedroom.

For a few moments, Gus became very clear. He looked around at each of us, then at the chaplain, seemingly surprised at this gathering.

"Am I dying?" he asked the chaplain, who was holding his hand.

"Yes, Gus, barring a miracle, we think you are," he answered gently.

Gus looked the clergyman straight in the eye and thought for a long moment.

"Aw, shit!" he said.

The family spent the next few hours with Gus, caressing him and reminiscing about happier times together, as he quietly slipped into a coma and died.

Perhaps this story doesn't sound like a triumph, but for Gus to have died experiencing the anguish of the unspeakable things he had done in Vietnam would have been a tragedy. His only request for help easily could have been missed, buried as it was in a jumble of confused cries. It would have been easier to sedate him until the cries stopped. But whose needs would have been met—those of the observers, who were having to deal with the discomfort of watching Gus's anguish, or Gus, who needed to be forgiven so he could die peacefully?

We have described reconciliations sought with others. Theresa and Sheila needed healing of relationships with other people. Arthur and Gus needed reconciliation with God. But there's another kind of reconciliation. People may feel that some aspect of their behavior is ethically or morally inconsistent with their values or standards. This affects their relationship with themselves. If they feel sad, troubled, or guilty about some behavior, incident, or circumstance, they cannot feel at peace.

ANNE

An Englishwoman living alone in America, Anne had a hospice nurse with a similar background. They often reminisced about growing up in England and shared stories of adjusting to life in the United States.

Anne was in her late forties but looked much younger, and seemed naïve. She often expressed surprise at how her life had turned out—that she was "in such a state," as she said, referring both to her illness and to her personal life.

She had worked for years in a small bakery, and had become romantically involved with the owner. Mr. Brown was married, but Anne had believed him when he talked of getting a divorce and marrying her. However, nothing came of it, and she slipped into the pattern of secrecy he demanded. He paid her rent, she continued to work at the bakery, and their affair went on for more than ten years.

Then Anne became ill with cervical cancer. She often needed time off from work; she was grateful that her boss told her to take all the time she needed. But as she became more ill, she needed more help, and he became less willing. When she asked him to take her to the doctor's office because she was too weak to drive, or to pick up a few things from the store, he refused.

Anne's feelings about him alternated between affection and loathing. Most of all she felt embarrassed and humiliated. She was ashamed to be involved with a married man, and mortified by the way he treated her. He had insisted that she tell no one of their liaison; and combined with Anne's natural shyness this command had left her friendless. She had no one to turn to except him, and he'd become distant, willing to extend himself only as far as might seem appropriate for an employer concerned about a valued employee's health.

Anne tried to maintain the secret. We helped her plan for the time when she no longer would be able to care for herself. She wanted to go into a nursing home, so Mr. Brown wouldn't have to help with her care, or feel responsible for her. And no one need know of their relationship.

A nursing-home placement was being planned when Anne suddenly became worse. She was much weaker, having increased pain and bleeding, and her speech was disjointed and difficult to follow. While rambling about pain, bandages, and cranberry juice, she became upset and tearful.

"Do you remember how they used to dig the bodies out of the rubble after the air raids?" Anne asked. "Do you remember all the red double-decker buses? Do you think there will be a bus for me soon?"

Thinking Anne might be trying to say she was dying, the nurse asked if that was what she meant.

"Yes, but I have to get to the other bus stop!" Anne said, getting more upset.

"Would you like to move to the nursing home soon?" the nurse asked.

"Yes," Anne sighed. "The bus can stop there."

Arrangements for the nursing home were speeded up, and by that evening Anne had been moved. She was calm and relaxed during the ambulance ride. At the home, she seemed a little flustered by the attention she received, but soon settled into her new bed, took her usual pain medicine, and went to sleep. The next morning her hospice volunteer visited and found Anne lying quietly, at peace, and taking her last few breaths.

Anne had wanted the bus to stop for her—to die—at the nursing home so no one would know of her clandestine relationship. If her message had gone unheard, would she have died that night? Could she have died peacefully in the apartment, or would she have become more agitated, worrying about being exposed? Those who knew her in her last days have no doubt that she died more easily knowing she had avoided being a source of embarrassment to anyone.

JANINE

At forty-two, Janine was a talented painter, prolific and successful. She and Jeff were unmarried—her ex-husband refused to divorce her—but lived together in a beautiful twenty-second-floor apartment. They delighted in the panoramic views. Janine was best known for her cityscapes and often painted from her balcony.

Unconventional and strong-willed, she wasn't willing to consider defeat, though she knew her pancreatic cancer was too advanced for a cure. She went through every possible traditional treatment, then opted to try some nonapproved treatments in Mexico.

By the time she contacted hospice she was in the hospital, in an advanced stage of her illness, and extremely fragile. Realizing she would die soon, she dreamed of returning to her apartment to live out her last weeks with Jeff as she looked out over her beloved city.

Jeff was very eager to take her home but the task seemed impossible, as her care was too complex for him to manage. Many of her symptoms were out of control. She had open wounds that needed frequent dressing changes, she was being sustained on intravenous fluids, she was unable to get out of bed, and too weak to manage any of her personal needs.

It was decided that she would benefit by being admitted to the hospice inpatient unit in the hopes of simplifying her care and teaching Jeff how to manage it. With much to do and time running out, the staff was concerned that Janine might die before they could achieve these goals. Happily, they did achieve them.

The night before the ambulance was to take Janine on her last trip home, another nurse and I were visiting her to check that all was in order. Jeff was about to leave for home with the flowers and other belongings that had accumulated. We were giving Janine a pep talk, reassuring her that everything was ready and that she would soon be enjoying the city lights. We were scooting her up in the bed and smoothing her pillows when we noticed the glassy, faraway look in her eyes.

"I can see through the window to the city of lights across the river!" she whispered with a radiant smile. We looked at each other with concern. Catching up with Jeff, we explained that such visions of a beautiful place beyond our awareness sometimes mean death is imminent.

"Don't go, Jeff," we said. "She may be dying tonight. Stay here with her."

But Janine didn't die that night. She lived another three weeks. During that time she gave us more messages of things that she needed for her death to be peaceful.

In Janine's fragile condition, transferring her home from the hospice inpatient unit was an enormous undertaking. Having met this request, we felt certain she would die peacefully and very soon. Everyone involved in her care became concerned when she was not peaceful, but instead restless and seemingly confused.

Her dying dragged on. We frequently asked ourselves what was missing—what she needed to die peacefully.

It was difficult to find any clear message in her disjointed mutterings. Looking for phrases or words that seemed significant, we realized that Janine was often saying "rings."

Could that be the key? If so, what did it mean?

"I suspect she means wedding rings," Jeff said sadly. "Janine has never felt comfortable with us living together without being married. We both desperately wanted to marry, but when Janine left her husband, he was in such a rage, he refused to agree to a divorce. When enough time had gone by legally for Janine to divorce him she'd already been diagnosed with her cancer and he threatened to declare her mentally incompetent due to the extent of her illness. And, you know, he's a lawyer, so he could probably get away with it!

"You can imagine the sorrow this mess has caused Janine."

Considering this information, we decided to call the chaplain to request a visit.

"Sweetheart, the chaplain's coming by this evening," Jeff told Janine. "Remember how much you've enjoyed his visits? Maybe he can help us all find some peace and comfort."

Janine didn't respond.

The chaplain was familiar with Janine and Jeff's situation.

"Jeff, Janine may need some special recognition of the commitment you and she have made to each other as a couple," the chaplain said. Jeff agreed. He and the chaplain explained to Janine that they were planning a special ceremony for the two of them. Friends would be coming to add to the celebration.

We weren't sure that Janine understood, but Jeff helped me dress her in her favorite nightgown, put flowers in her hair, and fix up her room. Friends were called. Jeff rushed out and bought wine and cheese.

Twilight was fading; the city lights were twinkling when the chaplain announced to those gathered that he would perform a ceremony to "bless this loving commitment." Obviously, he couldn't marry them—Janine was still legally married—but as he led the group in joyful hymns, Jeff tearfully slipped a ring on Janine's thin finger. Her restlessness ceased, and although she didn't speak, a tear slipped down her cheek.

When the celebration was over, the guests kissed and congratulated Janine and Jeff and said their good-byes. We padded the bedrails with pillows and made room for Jeff to lie in bed with Janine and cuddle her. It was their first peaceful night in three weeks. Early the next morning as the new light of dawn cast a gentle glow over the city, Janine died quietly in Jeff's arms.

When I saw Jeff at Janine's funeral, I gave him a big hug.

"I hope you know what a wonderful job you did, Jeff," I said. "No other hands could have cared for her as lovingly as yours did."

"Caring for her wasn't hard," he said. "Watching her suffer inside was. She was holding on for our wedding. I know that in the eyes of the church and the law we never married, but in our hearts we did. As much as I hated to let her go, I'm so glad we figured out how to give her the peace she needed."

The realization of the need for reconciliation that is part of Nearing Death Awareness seems to be similar to the effect of "seeing one's whole life pass before one's eyes" encountered in some near-death experiences. In both circumstances, people focus on relationships; Nearing Death Awareness seems to enable people to identify those aspects of relationships that make them feel sad, guilty, or troubled. To die peacefully, they need to effect some reconciliation or healing, whether by offering an apology or expressing gratitude. Sometimes the issue is mending ties to someone who has become estranged; sometimes reconciliation hinges on repairing something supposedly settled long ago, or which might appear insignificant to others.

One way to discover needs for reconciliation is to encourage a mental inventory of accomplishments and disappointments. This can be done orally, in the company of family and friends; or in writing, as a life history to be passed on to the next generation; or as letters to young children to be read when they're older.

Most dying people begin by listing their accomplishments, but they also will consider disappointments—tasks not completed, opportunities missed, relationships broken or left to wither. As caregivers or friends, if we can help dying people condu t such reviews and heal damaged relationships, we can help them find peace.

Most people, as they're dying, want to feel that their having been alive has been significant, that they made some difference in this world and in the lives of those around them. For all of us, some periodic review of how our lives are going, and recognition of our achievements, may help us find more enjoyment and purpose in our lives. At the same time some recognition of our "unfinished business" or troubled relationships may lead us to try to heal some problem areas now, rather than waiting until we are dying. This could enrich our lives and prevent frantic attempts at reconciliation when it is almost too late.

CHAPTER TWELVE

BEING HELD BACK: "I'M STUCK IN BETWEEN..."

Initially we had difficulty understanding how the messages of "Being Held Back" fit into the overall pattern of Nearing Death Awareness. Although these messages seemed to relate to several of the themes we've discussed, they were different, and required a category and explanation of their own.

Such messages are usually brief—sometimes little more than a phrase—but still convey clearly the sense that some of our patients are "stuck" somehow, or thwarted in their efforts to move on to a peaceful death.

As we looked closely at their messages, we found that although the words used resembled those in other categories, these patients were being "held back" by something still undone. These unresolved issues usually were related to a need for reconciliation—to finish unfinished business.

Telling us about "being held back" is a way dying people have of asking us to "look again—something's been missed!"

BERTHA

There was no shortage of people to care for Bertha; seven grown children, their spouses, and a flock of grandchildren were involved, as were friends from her church. Her tiny apartment seemed always full of different faces. Neighbors from the housing project would ask me how Bertha was doing as I passed them in the hallway. Despite the poverty in which she and her neighbors lived, there was an abundance of love and attention for Bertha. She was deteriorating steadily but seemed peaceful and comfortable, so I was surprised one day to find her restless and anxious.

"I can't find the feed for the horses!" she complained.

"Why do the horses need feed?" I asked. She looked at me as if I were crazy.

"I'd *never* make them take me on this trip without feeding them first!" she answered. Her indignation was apparent, but she was unable to tell me more.

"I understand," I said. "And I'll try to help you find what you need."

I repeated this brief conversation to Bertha's granddaughter Tanya, who smiled and said, "Granny's living in the past. She grew up on a farm back in the hills of North Carolina. All they had for getting around was a horse and wagon."

I suggested that this might be Granny's way of trying to tell us that she needed something in order to be peaceful in her dying.

"Do you have any idea what it might be?" I asked.

"Has anyone told you about Dwayne?" Tanya said.

"No, I've never heard that name," I said. "Is he a member of your family?"

Tanya explained that Bertha had eight grown children, not seven. "But nobody counts Dwayne!" she said with disgust. "He's been nothing but trouble—in and out of jail. He's broken Granny's heart more times than I can count, and now the bum won't even come and see her.

"The others don't want him here, anyway! He only comes around when he wants something and they feel like he's used Granny. I personally think he's feeling bad: he's been sending money to pay for her medicines. I'll bet he's trying to fix *his* bad feelings."

I suggested that Bertha might need to see her prodigal son. Some family members resisted at first, but agreed to contact

Dwayne, who was willing to talk to the hospice social worker as an intermediary.

Dwayne told her that he stayed away out of guilt for the sorrow he'd caused his mother and because he felt rejected by his siblings. A family conference was called and the decision was made "to give Dwayne one more chance for Mom's sake."

The reunion was heart-wrenching. Dwayne held his frail, thin mother in his big, strong arms and sobbed, "I'm sorry! I'm sorry!" Bertha stroked his face and with tears in her eyes whispered, "Jesus loves you, son, and so do I."

His siblings' hostility toward Dwayne when he arrived gradually changed to tolerance, then cautious acceptance as they watched his tender behavior toward his mother.

During the next two weeks Dwayne and Bertha spent quiet hours together, until she peacefully died, never having mentioned horses or feed again.

BEN

As his illness progressed, Ben, a former streetcar mechanic, became more dependent on others. At the same time his wife continuously reminded us of her own needs.

"Don't forget, I have a weak heart!" Lucy, eighty-two and obese, would say.

"I've never been a strong person!" she'd wail. "My doctor says stress and worry are bad for me! I don't know what Ben expects from me—he's just being selfish. I'm not a well person myself!"

Ben would shake his head sadly.

Lucy's apparent lack of caring and sympathy for her dying husband was difficult for everyone to understand. The more nursing help we put in their home, the more she wanted, and the less she did for Ben. With her lack of willingness to be involved in any part of his care, it became necessary for us to suggest that Lucy either hire additional nursing help or put Ben in a nursing home. She wouldn't hear of the latter.

"We don't have that kind of money," she snapped. "And what would my friends think if I put him in a home?"

Ben's use of symbolic language was in keeping with his earlier life as a worker on the mass-transit system in the city.

"That damn trolley keeps going right by," he'd say, "and won't stop for me!"

"It will, Ben, it will," I said, wondering how long it would take before he would find the peace he needed. The picture of a tired old man standing alone in the cold, waiting patiently at the platform only to have the trolley pass him by each time, was poignant. How lonely he must have felt!

Despite our gentle and repeated explanations about the seriousness of Ben's condition and that he might die soon, Lucy's anger at his leaving her was so strong that she could not, or would not, be with him. Lucy only saw Ben as a confused man who was "already out of it."

Sadly, we were never able to work through the walls she built around her anger. Each of our efforts was met with a litany of her own needs and with annoyance at Ben. His confusion became her justification for distancing and protecting herself from his dying, and from her own feelings of grief and fear.

Ben mentioned the trolley again with sadness and frustration.

"Ben, that trolley *will* stop for you soon," I said. "And you'll be able to go. The nurse will stay with you, so you won't be alone. But Lucy doesn't seem able to understand that it's time for you to leave, and it's too hard for her to be here with you— she's probably afraid. The social worker will work with her now, and even after you're gone, to make sure she's all right."

He nodded sadly.

Over the next few days, Ben became increasingly withdrawn and had little to say. There was no more mention of the trolley. He died quietly and sadly with the nurse holding his hand while Lucy remained in the next room, engrossed in her television program.

Ben knew that we understood his sorrow and had tried to help Lucy respond to his need for her. He must have felt some comfort knowing that we would try to help Lucy deal with her grief and fears of being alone. It wasn't what he had asked for, but it gave him some assurance, so he could get on with his dying. Ultimately, we can only offer suggestions for how it could be better, but we can't always make it so.

Both Ben and Bertha used the language of travel or change— "the trolley keeps going by . . ." and "the horses need feed for this trip." But the real message was "I need reconciliation."

Ben needed his wife to move past her anger, so he could die feeling that she wasn't rejecting him for dying. He needed her to move beyond her own pain so that she could be closer to him as he dealt with his.

And Bertha needed to reconcile her relationship with her lost son and see him accepted back into the family before she could leave in peace.

CHARLES

Charles was ready to die. For eighteen months his cancer had been spreading; he'd had enough of catheters, of dressings, of pain medicines. He'd told anyone who visited he was sure death would mean peace, and a closer connection to God.

"This can't go on forever, can it?" he asked his doctor. "I'm ready to have some peace."

"Not much longer," the doctor said, and Charles seemed relieved at first. But later he became disoriented and upset. His wife, troubled by the change, called and asked me to visit.

"I can't understand what's happening," she told me. "He doesn't make sense!"

I found Charles distraught—sometimes tearful, sometimes angry, sometimes terrified. When asked to tell us what was going on, he only became more upset, descending into incoherence. We tried more pain medicine, but that didn't help; neither did sleeping pills or sedatives.

His wife, Marie, and I looked for possible causes of his discomfort. Little that Charles said made sense, except the phrase "I can't go." I wondered if something might be stopping him from dying peacefully, but no one could think what it might be.

Three days passed, during which the sedatives gave Charles brief periods of troubled rest; when awake, however, he struggled and raved. Marie stayed right with him, seeming to share his agony, wishing she could ease it, and then heard him say, "John." When her husband groaned the name, she became deeply unsettled.

"He hasn't talked about John for years," she said. John, their oldest son, had killed himself. In his late teens, he'd begun a pattern of heavy drinking and violent outbursts, terrorizing his parents. Once, Charles had found John hitting Marie, and called the police. After that, John accumulated a series of arrests for drunk driving and fighting. In his suicide note, he blamed his father, claiming that his first arrest had sent him down the path of self-destruction.

"I was willing to forgive and forget, but Charles could never forgive John for hurting me," Marie said. "Why would he be talking about John now?"

There was no indication that Charles felt John was present; in fact, in a moment of coherence, Charles said John wasn't and hadn't been there.

The family minister wondered if Charles might want to resolve the relationship with John. Maybe he needed to forgive his son, maybe he needed to pray, asking his son's forgiveness? Charles became more upset at these suggestions and appeared terrified.

Marie and the minister spent hours with Charles trying to clear up the mystery, but nothing came clear until she mentioned that the anniversary of John's death was approaching. The minister focused on this when talking with Charles. He concluded that Charles feared that if he died on that date John would be there to meet him. The minister assured Charles that he'd find peace after death, not anger; John too was probably at peace; he couldn't hurt Charles or Marie anymore.

As the anniversary neared, this conversation recurred three or four times a day—each time Charles would be calm for a time, until his agitation rose and Marie would call the minister.

This pattern held until the anniversary passed, when Charles woke early, spoke weakly about being tired and ready to find some peace, and began a rapid deterioration. He died quietly that evening.

The key to his discomfort—"I can't go"—may have had its roots in troubled memories of John; the minister's repeated assurances were what were needed to help John through this trying time.

CLAUDE

"People have always teased Claude about being compulsive," his wife, Emily, said. "But he's just a very conscientious person who pays attention to detail."

Their spotless and tidy home was a testimony to their organized lives. Claude's favorite pastime was writing new programs for his home computer.

Before becoming ill with melanoma, Claude had worked long hours as an accountant, yet managed to donate his free time to help housebound senior citizens in the community with their taxes and health-insurance claims.

"The system is just too confusing for a lot of them," he said. He was a modest, gentle, and generous man, who dealt with his terminal illness as he had dealt with his life—in a quiet, noncomplaining, organized manner.

Claude's condition was deteriorating rapidly as the Christmas holidays approached; for no apparent reason, his peacefulness was replaced by agitation and confusion.

"I can't find the program," he said. "So the system won't work!"

"You will, and we'll try to help you any way we can," I assured him. Like many people, he wasn't able to say more.

Emily and I talked at length about the sense that something was holding Claude back.

"What is missing that would give him the peace he once had?" I asked.

Emily was at a loss to explain, as were their adult children. As a family they'd all worked together providing help and emotional support for Emily and participated in the care Claude needed. They'd done a wonderful job and had given Claude permission to "let go and go with it." They were not aware of any unfinished business; they'd assured him they were ready for his leaving, would stick together to help Emily, and would be all right. Nothing seemed to have been left undone.

An unexpected call from one of Claude's business partners provided the answer. He telephoned to assure Emily that, some months before, Claude had arranged for him to handle any financial matters. Emily tearfully told him that Claude was close to dying.

"What a shame!" he said. "He's just the greatest! And he was so worried he'd die before the new year."

"Why?" Emily gasped.

"If he could hang on past the first of the year, his retirement benefits would move into a higher category of payments for you," the partner said.

Emily was thunderstruck; she'd had no idea.

She and the children reassured Claude that he'd been a good husband and father, and had provided well for Emily's financial future. But no one was surprised when Claude lingered and died quietly on January 2—with higher retirement benefits for Emily.

Charles and Claude presented their needs in the impatient or frustrated manner that some people do, when something is delaying them or holding them back. It's the message that something is missing or unfinished that makes "Being Held Back" slightly different from the other themes. Charles was thwarted by the fear that he might have to relive his son's violence again. The basis of Claude's struggle was the desire to die after his retirement benefits increased for his wife. Once these issues of unfinished business were resolved, both were able to achieve peaceful deaths.

BILL

Bill, twenty-seven, was dying of AIDS. His father hadn't spoken to him for three years, ever since Bill had told his folks he was gay. A third bout of pneumonia in four months had left Bill without appetite or energy; at five feet eleven, he weighed less than a hundred pounds. His mother pleaded with him to come home, knowing he was too ill to be alone in his apartment.

"I'd like that," Bill said. "But what about Dad?"

"Don't worry, Son," she said. "I'll work it out with your father."

But she couldn't make it work.

"If you bring him home, I'm leaving!" the father said. When his wife told him she was bringing Bill home on Friday morning, the older man made good on that threat and left.

Bill was not expected to live more than a day or two, and when comfortably settled at home he said, "I'm ready to die now, I'm so tired of living like this." He was physically comfortable; three friends were helping his mother with his care. His priest came daily with communion, along with ice cream to tempt his appetite. Bill took communion but ignored the sweets. He talked with his priest about the situation with his father. The priest, Bill's mother, and I each called the father, asking him to visit. He refused, saying he didn't want to see his son or even hear his name. Bill was saddened by this but said, "I don't know why I thought it would be any different; he's been like this for years."

Bill became weaker, barely able to talk, occasionally smiling at his mother and friends or moving his lips as the priest prayed. Mostly he lay quietly, seemingly at peace and ready to die. But death wouldn't come. Tuesday morning his mother found him crying.

"Dad's in the way," he whispered.

"Do you want to see your father?" she asked. Bill tried to nod. Rather than phoning again, the priest went to see Bill's father at work. The priest told him his son was dying and begged him to visit.

"I don't think he can die peacefully without seeing you," he added. But the father rebuffed the plea. When the priest explained this, a deep sadness overcame Bill. He lingered two more weeks, often weeping, but never talking, except to say, "Dad's in the way." Finally, too exhausted to hang on, he died.

"Death isn't the worst thing that can happen to families," a neighbor said after Bill's funeral. "Estrangement can be worse."

ROSE

Rose and Eddie had been a close and religious couple, so she was distressed at his new and uncharacteristic hostility toward God.

"How can a loving God allow such a good woman to suffer?" Eddie would rage.

A minister helped him deal with these thoughts, but Rose suspected that Eddie remained angry at God. She worried that his anger was blasphemous and would keep him out of heaven.

"I need a push!" she said to me, just hours before her death.

I spoke with Eddie, reminding him of the caring and supportive things he'd done to make Rose's dying easier. Then I asked him what he thought might be missing, as her comment intimated that something was. I wasn't surprised at his answer.

"I think she's worried about my anger at God," he said. "She has always had a strong faith and never felt angry at Him for her suffering and dying, like I do."

I asked him if he could help Rose with her sadness.

Eddie sat by her bed. "Now you listen, Rose," he said stroking her cheek with tears brimming in his eyes. "I really do love God; He's given us a long and happy life together. But I think He understands my anger—it's because I hate losing you so much! So don't you worry, honey. When my time comes I know He'll let us be together in Heaven!"

"Oh, Eddie!" she said with a smile.

When she died, shortly thereafter, I held Eddie as he sobbed, "I hate losing her! I just hate it!"

Clearly, what Rose needed was the assurance that her husband still loved God despite his anger at Him. Because of Eddie's words, Rose believed they would be reunited in the next life.

Both Bill and Rose were "being held back" by their need for a reconciliation—Bill's personal reconciliation with his father and Rose's need to be assured that her husband's spiritual relationship with God was not damaged by his anger.

The important message in "Being Held Back" is "I need something." Even with brief comments, dying people may be urging those around them to reexamine the situation and remedy that which has been missed—unfinished business, uncompleted reconciliation, or assurances of the family's preparedness. Resolving the problem may provide the dying an avenue to a peaceful death.

CHAPTER THIRTEEN

NONVERBAL COMMUNICATIONS: "MY ACTIONS SPEAK FOR ME."

Dying people have ways of communicating other than words; their behavior and actions are another way to show us what they're experiencing. It's common to see them reaching for someone or something unseen, smiling, waving, nodding, or weakly attempting to talk with someone invisible to others. They may pick at the bed linens as though trying to remove them, or try to get out of bed. When this happens, the person usually isn't frightened but often has a look of wonder, recognition, joy, and sometimes puzzlement.

Although these actions seem inappropriate, and are often interpreted as confused behavior, they indicate the person is experiencing something. That "something" is part of Nearing Death Awareness. This behavior is a nonverbal way of communicating experiences of dying, of showing that dying people aren't alone, that others who have died are meeting them. These reunions are not only with those with whom the dying have had long-term relationships, or with people from the recent past, but can be with anyone. These gestures give us glimpses of whatever dimension exists beyond the life we know, and show us how we might take comfort from these reunions and messages.

BRAD

Bright, handsome, kind and gentle by nature, Brad was an accomplished writer for a large advertising agency. Only thirty, he was far too young to die of anything, but especially of a tragic and ravaging illness. Suffering with the sudden and unpredictable ailments that come with AIDS, Brad in many ways personified the early days of the epidemic.

Brad and Adam, his partner of six years, shared a small, beautifully decorated townhouse in a city thousands of miles away from Brad's family home in Canada. Although Brad had pulled up stakes ten years before, he remained in close touch with his parents and brother, Lee, a commercial artist in Quebec. He called home every week and returned home each Christmas, always careful to conceal his sexual orientation and the degree of his closeness to Adam.

"They had no idea about our relationship or how sick Brad was," Adam told me. "He struggled for years with how and when to tell his family he was gay. They're really wonderful, caring people, but he anguished about it; he was afraid the truth would break their hearts."

When Brad first began to come down with the opportunistic infections often associated with AIDS, he minimized them to his parents during their weekly phone calls. But they became increasingly more concerned with each problem Brad reported.

"It seemed strange to me that he was sick so often," his father said later. "He'd always been such a strapping, healthy young man."

When his boss realized that Brad had AIDS he fired him, claiming it was a necessary reduction in the staff. The firing cost Brad his income and his health-insurance coverage.

"Can you imagine that?" Adam said, with growing anger. "Brad had been one of their best employees for eight years. How's that for loyalty? Of course they denied any discrimination against him because of his illness or sexual orientation. We thought about hiring a lawyer to see what could be done, but frankly we didn't have the money and Brad was getting too sick to deal with it. We didn't want the notoriety anyway."

Adam, a respected sports reporter for one of the city news-papers, wasn't able to add Brad as a dependent on his health insurance or even use sick leave to care for him. All he could do was work as much overtime as possible to help pay the bills—amid the daily grind of changing soiled sheets, bathing Brad, and giving his medicines.

"His medical bills are unbelievable," Adam said. "The cost of just one of his medicines—AZT—is staggering! I begged him to level with his folks and seek their help, but he refused."

When Christmas came and pneumonia kept Brad from re-turning home, the matter was taken out of his hands. Missing their younger son and concerned about his health, Brad's parents decided to surprise him with a visit. They drove from Canada and knocked on Brad's door, only to receive a double-barreled shock.

"When they heard the word 'AIDS' there was a stunned silence for what seemed like an eternity," Adam said. "Finally Brad's father stood up and said to his wife, 'I need some fresh air. Will you join me?' They left together.

"My heart was aching for Brad *and* his parents," he said. "It must have been awful for them, and I knew Brad was afraid they would never come back. But two hours later they returned, faces puffy from crying. It was so sad. They hugged us and said, 'We'd like to stay and help if that's okay with both of you.' I can't tell you how relieved I was. Brad's eyes filled with tears."

The next few days were spent rearranging the den to make room for Brad's parents. His father called his business associate, explaining he'd be taking an indefinite leave of absence. His mother arranged for neighbors in Canada to watch their house and forward their mail. When Lee learned of his parents' plans, he offered to drive down the following weekend to bring addi-tional clothing for his folks and some of his artwork for Brad's bedroom walls.

But sometimes love and family support aren't enough. Brad's condition was changing rapidly; he no longer could manage the trip to his doctor's office. His physician encouraged Adam and Brad's parents to consider hospice home care, as Brad needed regular monitoring by professionals. They agreed.

"Brad's so sick now that he can't be left alone at all," Adam said on my first visit. "I don't know what we would have done if his parents hadn't offered to stay. But we all need help and suggestions about taking care of him."

Brad quickly became bedridden and couldn't care for himself at all. The AIDS virus was affecting his brain. Confused, unable to speak, and possibly deaf, he'd fix his big brown eyes intently on whoever was near him, and follow that person with a look of urgency—as though he had something important he wanted to say.

We always spoke to him, explaining everything we were doing, assuming he could hear and understand. He rarely reacted, but we had a strong sense that he was aware of everything and everyone around him.

As the weeks and months passed, my admiration for Brad's parents grew. They never questioned or showed anger at this tragedy. They simply loved their son while gently and tirelessly providing for his every need. A mutual respect and love grew between them and Adam, as they worked together caring for Brad.

Becoming more debilitated, he stopped being able to swallow, but was receiving some fluids intravenously. We became concerned that these extra fluids might be prolonging his suffering and dying, rather than improving the quality of his life.

The doctor explained to Brad's parents that the IV fluids might delay his death by a few days, but that he was no longer really benefiting from them. He said the extra fluid might strain Brad's failing circulatory system, and recommended they be discontinued. This was a very upsetting and difficult change for Adam and Brad's parents to consider.

Our need to nurture is intense. We survive, thrive, and grow; we comfort, celebrate, and reward ourselves—and the people we care about—with food and drink. For parents, this need is profound, regardless of the child's age. Providing nourishment for our children is an essential part of a parent's role. Withholding it feels like denying love and nurturing—the very core issues of parenting. So, despite the inability of dying people to tolerate or benefit from fluids and nourishment, families and friends agonize over the question of ending them.

Brad's parents didn't want to stop the IVs. Adam and the doctor supported their decision. "This is difficult enough for them," the doctor said. "Continuing the IVs at a minimal rate won't make much difference to Brad, but if that helps his parents, then so be it."

When I visited, a few days later, Brad wouldn't look at me at all. Despite numerous attempts, I could not get his attention. His eyes were fixed, glaring at the IV bag hanging on the pole above his bed.

"Brad, I know this is hard for you," I said, holding his hand. "I'll bet you're really sick of it all and would like it to be over. You look like you're angry at the IVs, but we have them running as slowly as possible, so as not to drag this out. But your parents don't want to stop the fluids, because they love you so much. It's a decision that's too painful for them."

As I finished speaking, Brad shifted his gaze from the IV bag to the wall opposite his bed, where Lee had hung a charcoal sketch several months before. He stared intently at that picture. I hadn't paid much attention to it before, but on this day its symbolism was striking.

Lee had drawn a study in shadows and light, showing an old stone bridge, arched over a long dark mountain tunnel, at the far end of which a brilliant white light gleamed.

Many people report going through a passageway toward a wonderful bright light during Near Death Experiences; people who are dying slowly often have such occurrences, as well. I returned to Brad's side and took his hand again, stroking it.

"Brad, if you're ready to go, it's okay," I said. "I'll explain to Adam and your parents what I think you're trying to tell us."

We gathered around his bed as I explained my interpretation of Brad's behavior. By looking at the picture—with its image of passage—I thought perhaps he was attempting to tell us the time had come for his journey. Tearfully they hugged and kissed him, giving him permission to go.

"We love you and we'll miss you, Brad," Adam said. "But

you've fought long enough and we're ready for you to go whenever you need to." Brad closed his eyes and relaxed.

During the next two days, Brad alternated between deep sleep and periods of being "glassy-eyed," seeming to look through us at something we could not see. Lee was called to come.

Everyone was restless, wandering in and out of Brad's room, taking turns napping and sitting with him. Touching and stroking him, they murmured soft reassurances. From deep sleep he drifted into a brief coma, barely noticed. He then quietly died with the people he loved around him.

At Brad's funeral, Lee said, "We were so close growing up we could almost read each other's minds. So it means a lot to me that he told us he was ready to die through my picture. It feels like I helped talk for him when he couldn't talk for himself anymore."

Unable to speak, Brad still could communicate his awareness that death was near. And, with help, his caregivers were able to understand his nonverbal message, giving him the permission he needed to go, and themselves the opportunity to prepare for his death.

At one of our recent workshops, a middle-aged man told us his mother had died the previous year. A stroke had left her in a coma for several weeks; but moments before she died, she awoke, broke into a beautiful smile, and reached for something unseen. She put her arms together and looked down joyfully, as if cradling a baby. She died in that posture with a look of happiness on her face.

There's a story behind this touching scene. The man explained that his mother's first baby had died just moments after birth. She went on to have five other children; all survived and grew into adulthood.

"We all knew Mother had lost a baby, but we never talked about it," he said. "From the look on her face, I *know* she died holding that baby again!"

. . .

Knowing that a dying person may be reunited with someone they cared about reinforces our hope that love and important relationships may be eternal. Many families take great solace from thinking the person they love is not alone while dying and after death, but in fact may be in the presence of spiritual beings, perhaps the Almighty.

ALAN

All through their marriage, Alan and Margaret had argued. When I first met them they were arguing about the soup she'd made for his lunch.

"It's the homemade vegetable soup he loves," Margaret said. "This morning that's what he said he wanted. So I went to the store and spent all morning making it, but he took one taste and now says he doesn't want it; he's not hungry. Can you believe that?"

I explained how a diminishing appetite is part of many illnesses—especially the cancer that Alan had—and suggested that he probably wasn't interested in eating.

"Oh, well," she said. "I didn't realize that. Then it's all right. I thought he was just trying to make my life difficult!" She laughed and bent over the bed to give Alan a quick hug.

I soon realized that arguing and physical contact were this couple's preferred methods of communication. Whenever Alan and Margaret were close enough to touch, they did—holding hands or hugging, even as I was examining Alan or asking about his symptoms. Often when I arrived I'd find Margaret curled up in bed with Alan, reading to him or watching television with him.

Even so, anything and everything was an occasion for an argument. They argued about whether or not Alan should get out of bed, whether he should take his medicines with ice cream or applesauce, which television programs they should watch. When I commented on this, Margaret said, "You know we've always been like this. I really love him and I know he loves me, but we both love to argue. It's never nasty and often not even serious. Sometimes I think it's the way we stay close, although I guess that might seem a little strange to other people.

"I tried to stop once," she said. "After he got sick I told him we'd do everything as he wanted, from now on. But he said, 'Listen, you don't have to be nice to me just because I'm dying! If you stop disagreeing with me I'll think I'm dead already! Besides, I love you just the way you are.' So I didn't change my ways—but now I let him win!"

Margaret was troubled that Alan had no belief in a life after death. "All the years we've been married we've disagreed about this," she said. "I go to church every week, but he's never come with me. He says he knows that when he dies that's the end— and that's all right with him. 'I've had a good life,' he tells me. 'I know you won't forget me, so I'll live on in your memories.'

"I don't think that's enough," Margaret said. "I wish he could believe the way I do, but he won't even discuss it."

Alan never did discuss religion, even to argue about it with his wife. He refused all offers of clergy and prayer and seemed to be at peace with himself.

For the last few days of his life Alan was in a coma, not talking or responding to anyone—not even to Margaret as she snuggled beside him.

One morning Alan's breathing changed while Margaret and I were with him. He opened his eyes and looked toward the far corner of the room. Smiling as if recognizing someone, he sat up in bed and reached out his arms. He sat that way for a few minutes, then closed his eyes, slowly dropped his arms, lay back, and died. Margaret was awestruck.

"I hoped he'd just stop breathing and die easily, and he did, but this . . ." she said, shaking her head. "It was as if he saw someone, and tried to reach for a hug. Who did he see? Could it have been Jesus? Have you ever seen this before?"

I told her about similar scenes I'd witnessed, and we talked about what Alan might have been seeing. Later, after the undertakers had removed Alan's body, Margaret and I were having a cup of tea when she suddenly laughed.

"Well, I won that argument, didn't I?" she said. "I told him we'd meet again and he said we couldn't because there wouldn't be anything after death. But he sure saw something we didn't, and he's gone somewhere else now. So he'll be waiting for me when I go and I'll be able to say, 'I told you so!' Do you think we can argue forever in Heaven?"

This seeing, smiling at, or reaching for someone we cannot see is the nonverbal form of the messages we described in Chapter 7, "Being in the Presence of Someone Not Alive." People respond to or reach for someone or something beyond our perception. When this happens, as with Alan, the person often has a look of wonder, recognition, and joy.

KAREN

Several years after Alan's death, I heard from Karen, who as a nursing student had been observing the team meeting the day I described what had happened to Alan. She had moved but called to tell me about the events during her mother's recent death from cancer. Her family had managed at home until the last few days when her mother went into the hospital, where she died three days later.

Her death was expected; in fact, the family had been hoping she'd die soon, feeling that she had suffered enough. But they were shocked to learn that she fell out of bed and was found dead on the floor.

"You can imagine how we felt!" Karen told me. "My dad was crying and cursing himself for going home. He said she wouldn't have fallen if he'd been there. My sister and I were almost crazy with guilt. She's a nurse, too, and of course we blamed ourselves for not keeping her at home. My brother was furious at the hospital staff! All of us were so distraught the nurse asked if we wanted to see the chaplain, who turned out to be a young woman.

"I knew exactly what my dad was thinking: 'How can this young girl know anything about this?' But she listened to us rant and rave, asked a few questions, and let us get out some of our pain and grief. After quite a long while she said, 'Do you think she could have been trying to go somewhere, maybe to meet her Maker?' "

"My dad looked stunned, my brother was skeptical, but I immediately remembered your story about Alan," Karen said. "I told them about it. The chaplain nodded and described other situations she'd seen—dying people opening their eyes, smiling, trying to reach for something or someone. My sister, who's been a nurse much longer than I have, recalled that she'd seen similar behavior, too.

"What's so interesting is how differently we all felt then about Mother's having fallen. Now we don't dwell so much on her struggling to get out of bed; instead, we remember that she was ready to die and that she believed—and we see her going home to her God."

Just before they die, and usually without warning, some patients can muster an unusual strength. Unfortunately, some use that strength to try to get out of bed, and subsequently fall. Afterward, the family feels a terrific amount of guilt, and may blame the fall for causing the death. A frightened and tearful family member may say: "Dad just died. He was trying to get out of bed and fell to the floor! We've been with him all the time, but I'd just run down to the kitchen for coffee. I feel just awful. It's my fault; if I'd been there this wouldn't have happened! How could this have happened, anyway? He's been semiconscious, barely responsive for the past two days, didn't even have the strength to hold a glass of water. He was too weak to move at all by himself! How could he get over the bed rails? I don't understand it! How can I live with this?"

Instead of assuming the worst, it's best to ask a few questions: What were the dying persons trying to do? Were they seeing someone or some place invisible to us? Were they trying to go there? Was someone that we couldn't hear calling them to come?

We certainly don't want to suggest that it's all right for dying people to fall out of bed. But no one knows the reasons for this phenomenon of reaching out—and sometimes climbing out of bed—in the last moments of life. The fall may not have caused the death; the person might have died at that time, whether he fell or not. The fall may have resulted from his response to something he was experiencing while dying.

Family members should understand this and be vigilant. But it's cruel to blame themselves for something that wasn't their fault or due to their negligence because they didn't understand that dying people can exhibit a final burst of energy. And it's always worth considering the hidden meanings behind the fall, so as not to miss the important messages in this type of nonverbal communication.

CHAPTER FOURTEEN

SYMBOLIC DREAMS:

"I DREAMED ABOUT..."

Dreams can be fascinating. People communicate with themselves through dreams, their unconscious minds bringing material to the attention of their conscious selves. In recounting dreams, people also communicate with others.

People who develop Nearing Death Awareness know they're not dreaming when they see a place or beings that others cannot—the messages about what dying is like—but dreams may help communicate about the second part of Nearing Death Awareness—what they need to die peacefully.

We are not experts in dream analysis, but we do have considerable experience listening to dying people's dreams, and know they often can be significant.

The dreams of someone facing a terminal illness often relate to strong emotions, and contain clues about important needs. By listening carefully, we can help people explore those needs and feelings and sometimes find solutions.

BECKY

Becky, a reporter in the Washington office of a major newspaper, was thirty-four. She lived with her husband, Joel. They had two big dogs that always escorted me into the bedroom and, as

Becky said, "supervised" everything I did. If I went into the den with Joel or to the phone in the kitchen, one would accompany me; the other would stand guard at the foot of Becky's bed.

Becky was a warm, quick-witted woman whose sense of humor remained strong even when the rest of her energy diminished. However, on my first visit she seemed anxious and wary. She knew she was dying.

"I know things don't look very promising for me," she said. "My doctor's been telling me for weeks that I should call the hospice. I guess there's nothing more that can be done."

She said her reluctance to call was because she thought having hospice meant that she'd have to talk about dying.

"You know, the doom-and-gloom approach," she said. "I could write a story about other people dying. I could find out everything about them—how they feel, what they do—but when it comes to me I don't want to discuss any of it."

"We'll try to make this time as comfortable as it can be," I said. "If you want to discuss dying, I'll be here. But I won't try to make you talk about anything you don't want to talk about."

"Then let's not talk about it, let's just have a good time!" she said. "I think we'll get along fine. I can see the dogs approve of you!"

I laughed; one of the dogs sighed loudly and sat on my foot, and the other was leaning his shaggy golden head against my skirt.

"Good," she said. "We'll have laughter instead of tears!"

We quickly grew to like one another. She often asked general questions about other dying people—newscaster Frank Reynolds had died recently—saying, "This question is off the record. I just want some background information."

About a month after I started visiting, I sensed something different about Becky. Joel ushered me into the bedroom, then left me alone with her.

"I'd better leave," he said. "Becky has something she wants to discuss with you."

Becky looked very serious. She patted the bed for me to sit beside her, and took my hand.

"I have to tell you about this dream I had last night—I guess it was a dream. I don't usually remember dreams but this was so real," she said. "I had a dream. . . . I had a tape recorder. . . . I was supposed to be interviewing someone, but I didn't know who it was. The recorder kept running . . . but nothing had been said, and I started to feel upset."

She was silent for a minute or two, then said, "I suddenly realized I was supposed to be interviewing Frank Reynolds, and I couldn't think of what to ask him. I woke up feeling very upset that the tape was going to run out and I still hadn't asked him anything. What do you think all this means?"

"I have a feeling you have an idea about that yourself," I said. "Can you tell me what you make of it?"

"I don't seem to be able to say anything today," she said. "Can you help me?"

"What did you think of Frank Reynolds?"

"Well, he was one of the best," she said. "He was so professional, so well prepared, but he was also very personable."

"I have the sense that if there was something you wanted to know and you could call up anyone at all to ask for answers, he might be the one," I said. "Is that possible?"

Becky's eyes twinkled. "Well, he was the best," she said, with a smile. "I always like the best."

"And what would you want to interview Frank Reynolds about?" I said.

"You'll have to tell me," she answered. "Suddenly I don't seem to be any good with words."

"Maybe you're wondering about dying and what it's going to be like," I said. "He just died, so he should be able to tell you. He's someone you respect, so you'd love to have the chance to find out from him what it's all about. If you're afraid of dying, would interviewing him be a way to find out if there's anything to be scared of?"

Becky was quiet for a few minutes, holding my hand tightly. "But I'm not dreaming now, and he's not here," she said, her voice trailing off, her eyes calm and serious and fixed intently on mine.

"Can I try to give you some answers?" I said.

"Yes, but I don't know the questions."

Asking her to stop me at any time if she wanted to, I started to talk about death. I described how people usually become weaker, slip into a coma, stop breathing, and die. I asked her if she wanted to hear more. She nodded. I told her what I thought her death would be like—probably the same drifting into coma and easy death. I mentioned that many people fear dying because they don't know much about it. I told her about specific fears about death, especially about suffering. I related this to her condition and said her pain probably would continue, but that we'd keep it controlled, as we had so far. Then I said some people had concerns about what happens after death.

"No, that's not it," Becky said.

Then she was quiet for a few minutes before smiling again. "Thank you, I feel better," she said. "That dream was the biggest interview of my life and I thought I blew it, but I got the information after all. Would you explain to Joel?"

Becky never talked about death again. Our conversation about her dream seemed to help answer her questions and calm her fears.

People's needs can be similar, but the way they express them, particularly in dreams, can be quite different.

JENNY

Jenny was nine years old and dying of brain cancer. One day she had a stroke that left her blind and paralyzed; from then on she deteriorated rapidly.

Her father, Matthew, was a diplomat. He and his wife, Pauline, came from the same small Ohio town but hadn't spent much time there in ten years. They had lived overseas for the most part. When Jenny became ill, Matthew was reassigned to Washington. Pauline was realistic about her daughter's illness. On my first visit she said, "All I ask now is that she doesn't have any pain and that she can die at home." They had decided not to give Jenny the details of her illness.

One morning I was showing Pauline how to wash Jenny's hair in bed. Jenny told us she'd had a dream the night before in which men wearing gray suits were taking her to a big ivy-covered house. She described the house in detail—red brick, polished wooden doors, ivy curling around the windows. As I was asking Jenny about the dream, Pauline began backing away, eyes wide and filled with tears. Saying she needed more towels, she left the room. Jenny continued to talk about her dream; I finished her hair. I asked how the dream made her feel.

"Well, I didn't know where I was, and who those men were, and where they were taking me," she said, looking very puzzled.

When I finished Jenny's hair she was tired, and settled down for a nap. In the other room I found Pauline and Matthew crying in each other's arms.

"That house she's talking about is the funeral home in Ohio where we're going to have her body sent," she said. "We decided to have her buried in the cemetery near my parents' home. Why is she dreaming about it?"

Pauline, Matthew, and I talked about the meaning of Jenny's dream. At first they wondered if Jenny could have overheard them talking about the funeral and burial. Then they remembered they had talked about the funeral home by name, not describing it. Jenny didn't know their hometown well, and had never been to the funeral home—or even near it—as far as they knew.

So what could the dream mean? I suggested they ask Jenny. Pauline was afraid Jenny would see how upset she was, and Matthew was concerned that Jenny might ask if he knew this place. I suggested perhaps we could identify how the dream made Jenny feel; recognizing the feeling behind a dream often reveals its meaning.

Pauline thought Jenny seemed puzzled, but not afraid. Could she mean she needed to know what was going to happen to her? Matthew and Pauline agreed it might be worth letting their daughter talk about what was puzzling her. They asked if I would call their minister, whom Jenny loved, so he and I could talk with her together.

The next day their minister and I visited Jenny. He asked how she was.

"Fine," she said.

"That's what you always say, but really, how are you doing?" he said.

"I think I'm getting worse," Jenny said. "I can't see, my right arm and leg don't work, and my left one doesn't do much either. I can't even hold Teddy"—a stuffed bear that we rested on Jenny's pillow so she could stroke it with her cheek.

"So there are lots of changes," I said. "And they all make it seem like you're getting worse, is that right?"

Jenny nodded.

"Do you wonder what's going to happen?" the minister asked.

"I think I'm going to die," she said. "What do you think?"

"Well, only God can know for sure," he said. "But from what you're telling me and what I see, I think you might. Do you want to talk about that?"

"Yes, but I didn't know who to ask," Jenny said. "I thought it might upset Mom and Dad; sometimes after they think I'm asleep I hear them crying."

"Tell us what you want to know," he said.

"Well, I'm not scared to be dead, I think I understand about that. The part of me that loves Mom and Dad will go to Heaven, right?" Jenny said. "And then my body will get buried. But what about before I die, what'll it be like for me? And what about Mom and Dad, will they be all right afterward?"

I described what I thought would happen: how she'd get weaker and not want to talk, smile, eat, or drink, and that then she wouldn't even feel like breathing, and her breathing would stop. I told her it wouldn't hurt, because we'd continue to give her medicine to relieve any pain. She asked if either of us had seen people die, and if it looked difficult. We said it looked like it was easy, that sometimes dying people seem to have relatives or friends who already have died there with them.

"No angels?" she said. "Can't I have an angel?"

The minister laughed. "Jenny, if you want an angel, I'm sure you'll have one," he said.

Jenny lived two more months, and died the way we had expected.

Afterward Pauline and Matthew talked about Jenny's dream. Understanding it helped them understand what she needed. As she was dying, she had been remarkably unafraid, and they were sure her conversation with me and the minister had eased her fears. After kissing her daughter's cheek, Pauline said, "I think I'll put Teddy in the coffin with Jenny. But I know she won't be lonely; I'm sure she's found an angel by now."

Identifying the feelings—for Becky, frustration, and for Jenny, feeling puzzled—lead to the same need: information, which we had and could share with them. Sometimes the dream's meaning isn't what we think at first, and the need cannot always be met.

LAWRENCE

Lawrence was sixty-eight, and dying in the hospice inpatient unit. He told me his dream as I was giving him a back rub, part of his night-time ritual—a warm washcloth for his face and hands, a toothbrush and mouthwash, and a back rub.

"It eases the stiffness in my back, so I feel relaxed and I'll sleep better," he said.

Although it certainly relaxed him, it rarely meant that he'd go to sleep; instead, it seemed to encourage him to talk, often for hours, about concerns he never mentioned in the daytime.

"I had such a vivid dream," he said. "I was in a circus tent, swinging up high on a trapeze. Down below I could see lots of people talking and laughing, and there were music and beautiful banners. But I kept swinging farther and farther. I knew that I could let go of the trapeze and I'd just keep going into what was out there. And out there it was cold and dark, lonely and empty—there was nothing."

We talked about what he thought the dream might mean.

"Well, down below in the tent is what being alive is like," he said. "It's people and noise and warmth, and beautiful colors. But out there where it's cold and lonely is death. That's what it's going to be like after I die—cold and lonely, and then nothing. I'll go through the cold and dark, and then I'll be nothing." We talked about the dream several times; I encouraged him to talk with others also.

After several nights of describing and discussing his dream, Lawrence realized it also described his life. His parents had been stern and undemonstrative. His wife had left him, telling him he was cold and unloving. His two sons weren't close to him; the younger one lived in California and visited only every few years, and although his older son lived in town he never came to see his father. Lawrence had no friends, only a few business associates.

"They had their secretaries send flowers when I first got sick, but they don't want to see me," he said.

When I asked what would make his life less lonely, he said he'd like to see his sons. The younger son did come, but after an awkward greeting the two seemed to have very little to say. The older son refused to visit his father.

Lawrence's dream at first sounded like a description of how his death would be, but really showed how he perceived his life. He was able to observe warmth and color and people and joy but never felt a part of it. The dream expressed his feelings of loneliness; and after some thought and discussion he was able to say what would relieve that loneliness. Unfortunately, the people he wanted and needed to help him couldn't. Those of us caring for him could empathize with his emotional pain, but we couldn't relieve it; he remained sad and lonely until his death.

Sometimes dreams cause feelings of fear; exploring those feelings can be particularly important.

ISABEL

Isabel, thirty-nine, was a psychologist. She had very complicated physical problems, and I visited her many times to teach her how to manage them. Her terminal neurological disease had progressed rapidly, ending her working days and much of her independence. Her younger brother, Edward, a poet, had moved in to help take care of her.

Isabel often mentioned the extra pressure she felt because of her profession.

"You have no idea how difficult it is to be a psychologist," she said. "My friends say it must be easier for me because I should know how to cope. But it's no easier for me than for anyone else. Dying is a new experience for me, and I'm as distressed and anxious as anyone would be. Even Edward asks me for advice about how he should deal with this, and he's supposed to be taking care of me."

One morning she said, "I need to talk about this terrible dream I had. I've had it every couple of weeks for the last few months. It was awful—I was buried alive!"

With a look of horror she described dreaming that she was in a coffin, unable to get out, feeling the weight of the earth pressing down on her.

"When I did wake up I was still so frightened that I was afraid to go back to sleep," she said.

Usually the best interpreter of any dream is the dreamer. I asked Isabel if she could explain her dream.

"Well, it reflects my anxiety, of course," she said. "I'm afraid the funeral director will take me away while I'm still alive! Then they'll put me in a coffin, take me to church for the service, then to the graveyard, and bury me. But what if I'm still alive?"

"That sounds pretty scary," I said.

"I'm the wrong kind of doctor for this," Isabel said. "I don't know much about death. How will you know that I'm dead? How can you be sure that I'm not still alive when the funeral director takes me away?"

The fear of being buried alive is not uncommon. Isabel understood what she needed to relieve her fear: she needed to know exactly how we'd determine she was dead, and she wanted the details. So we had the first of several discussions about how the heart and the lungs stop. I told her we'd try to find a pulse, at the wrist and in the neck, and then a blood pressure. We'd listen for a heartbeat, or for sounds of breathing. These are absent right after death. I said she'd remain at home for an hour or so after death, during which time other signs would appear. Her body would become cold; and as the blood stopped flowing, mottled blue patches would appear on the underside of her body.

These details may be too graphic for most people, but this is what Isabel needed to hear. They may sound too simple for someone of her background, but, like many people, Isabel had little experience with death. She wanted to know how many times I'd seen people die, and how often I'd examined those who had just died. I told her everything I could.

"Now I feel better," she said. "Talking about this has helped. I think my dreams were caused by anxiety about this. Maybe being a psychologist isn't so bad; at least I can figure out my anxieties."

On my next visit, her brother was on hand. Isabel asked if we could repeat our earlier discussion, but this time with Edward. So we talked again about Isabel's dreams, and her fear of being buried alive, and I described for Edward how we tell if people are dead.

"Now, Edward," said Isabel, "I want you to remember all this. Don't you go trying to hurry things up and get me out of here too quickly. Please keep me here at home for at least two hours after I'm dead. Don't rush me out."

Every few weeks over the next several months, Isabel asked to go over this topic; each time she seemed less anxious. The night she died Edward watched me check his sister's body for signs of life. As I finished and put away my stethoscope, he said, "I know Isabel's watching us to make sure we do everything we said we would. So I made some tea and I've got some choc-olate-chip cookies."

Edward and I spent two hours sitting with his sister, drinking tea and eating cookies, as he told me stories of their childhood.

After the funeral he said, "It never was easy for Isabel to

admit she was afraid of anything. I'm glad she told us what frightened her, and that we had all those weird conversations. At first it seemed ridiculous that I keep her home for two hours. But now it seems like such a little thing to have done, and I know it relieved her fears. It also helped me say goodbye."

A dying person's dreams may be very important. Pay particular attention to vivid dreams, recurring dreams, or a series of dreams that are progressive in some way.

If someone you know who is dying talks about dreams, he may be struggling with something he doesn't understand, but about which he has questions or strong feelings. Encourage him to tell you the details. Listen carefully. Ask him to interpret the dreams, but don't try to interpret them yourself. The most useful response is to try to help the person identify the feelings behind the dreams.

Dreams that frighten a person may relate to fears about illness or dying; dreams full of anxiety may mean a person is worried about family, expenses, or arrangements that need to be made. Dreams that are puzzling often indicate a need for information. Very often simply talking about their dreams helps the dying figure out what it is they are concerned about or need.

CHAPTER FIFTEEN

CHOOSING A TIME: "THE TIME IS RIGHT."

Some dying people realize they will die more peacefully under certain conditions; until those conditions are met, they may delay the timing of their deaths. This differs from knowing when they will die; some people *do* know and *do* indicate when death will happen, others actually choose the moment of death.

Some wait to die until certain people arrive, or until others leave, or until the ones they care about most have the right kind of support.

JOSEPH

Joseph carried himself like the career diplomat he'd been, but in forty years of holding posts around the world, he'd never put on airs. He and Dorothy, his wife of fifty years, had raised their two children in embassy compounds in half a dozen countries, collecting a string of languages, a houseful of unusual furniture and mementoes, and a lifetime of stories.

Patrick and Kathleen were grown and had gone on to have careers and young families of their own. Patrick, a teacher, lived in New York, and Kathleen, a nurse, lived an hour from her parents, but Joseph and Dorothy still had their big old wood-frame house and their memories of days in Italy, Arabia, England, Zanzibar, Japan, and China, among other exotic places.

After their wanderings, Joseph and Dorothy were content to stay at home. Both read voraciously; she preferred fiction, he liked political histories. Winter evenings they'd sit in the den beside a crackling fire and take turns recalling details from posts long past.

Joseph retired at sixty-five; three years later, he was diagnosed as having emphysema and heart disease. Neither condition was life threatening, but in the next nine years he gradually got sicker, experienced weight loss, weakness, and shortness of breath so severe he became totally dependent on Dorothy. His world shrank from the one he'd traversed by ship and airplane to a second-floor bedroom and the pages of *National Geographic* magazine. Tethered to an oxygen tank, he couldn't even join Dorothy by the fireplace to read and chat.

But at first Joseph didn't give in to the invalid's outlook. All his life he had dressed formally, and he still did so, insisting that every day Dorothy get him into shirt and tie and crisply pressed trousers, hanging them on a mahogany valet stand and inserting shoe trees into his well-polished shoes.

As Joseph's condition worsened, Kathleen and Patrick became more concerned about the burden his illness was placing on their mother. The old house rambled, with many steps between bedrooms and kitchen. Joseph never complained, but he too worried about his wife's frequent trips up and down the staircases.

"We've got to do something," he told Kathleen. "She needs help. This is too much for her."

Kathleen contacted the local hospice; for Joseph to be admitted, however, his doctor would have to certify that he had only six months or less to live. Joseph's doctor agreed that Joseph was failing, and acknowledged the family's concerns, but said he couldn't put a fixed length on his patient's future.

"He's been declining for such a long time, but he could go on like this for quite a while longer," the physician told Dorothy and Kathleen.

Dorothy hired a private-duty practical nurse to visit three times a week and help with Joseph's care and bathing, but the burden remained largely on her. The children lived out of state, worked full time, and had their own lives to manage. But the situation wore on them, too; each felt there was never enough time to do as much as was needed.

By now Joseph had lost so much weight that his face was sunken. His eyes had always been the most dramatic part of his face; now they were positively owlish. As his body fat disappeared, his bones became more prominent, not only giving him a skeletal appearance but increasing the risk of bedsores, caused by the pressure of an inactive body on tender skin. Joseph had never been a big or muscular man, but now he seemed fragile.

"When I help him out of bed those little bones feel as if they'll snap in my hand," Kathleen said.

His decline continued by degrees. He'd stopped dressing formally, and didn't seem to miss it. He spent less time in his chair by the bedroom window, he no longer read his *Geographics*, he tired quickly. Merely being around the grandchildren exhausted him. But he didn't want to be left alone. He'd call for Dorothy more often; when she'd appear and ask what he wanted, he'd say, "Don't talk. Just sit here." During a visit from Kathleen he grabbed his daughter's hand urgently.

"I'm not going to get better," he said. "I'm going to die."

"I know, Dad," Kathleen said. "I know."

One Sunday afternoon, as usual, Kathleen visited. Upon seeing her parents, however, she grew uneasy. Her mother was a bundle of nerves, and her father, who'd been bedridden for days, was having trouble swallowing. Kathleen called the doctor and asked if her father might be close to dying.

"It's possible," the doctor said. "Your father is physically fragile. On the other hand, he's been this fragile for a long time. It's really difficult to tell how much time he has."

Kathleen felt torn. As a nurse, she was well acquainted with the ups and downs of illnesses like her dad's, but worried about her own family and work responsibilities. She decided to go home.

But she fretted as each mile passed, fearing she might be missing her father's final evening of life, and at the same time caught up in practical matters—the disruption of patient visits set for the next morning, her own teenaged children's needs. She wished someone would tell her exactly what to do.

When Kathleen walked into the living room her children sensed her turmoil. Her daughter quickly settled the question.

"If you're going to be a wreck about it, Mom, you might as well be a wreck over there. Besides, Nana will like some company," she said.

That was all Kathleen needed to hear. She packed a change of clothing and drove back to her folks' house, planning to spend the night, get up early, and go to work as planned. As she opened the back door of the house, Dorothy rushed to embrace her.

"I'm so glad you came back," her mother said. "I didn't want to ask you to stay, but I've felt so nervous all day. Something's different about your father. I wish I could put my finger on it."

Upstairs, Joseph seemed startled at Kathleen's return. She smoothed the pillows and kissed him.

"Hi, Dad," she said. "I decided to spend the night so Mom wouldn't be alone."

Her father smiled with relief and reached for her hand.

"Good, now I can lie down," he said, closing his eyes.

Kathleen was puzzled by his comment; he'd been bedridden for a week. But she tucked him in and joined her mother downstairs for a cup of tea.

"I don't remember Dad being confused before," she said as they relaxed at the kitchen table. "He just said, 'Now I can lie down,' but that doesn't make sense. That's all he has been doing!"

"Maybe he was dreaming," Dorothy said. "We're both tired; nothing seems to be making much sense tonight. Let's get some sleep and maybe things will be clearer in the morning."

At dawn Dorothy awoke hearing Joseph as he tried to get out of bed.

"Joe, where are you going?" she asked.

"I want to lie down!" he said urgently. She got up and calmed him, persuading him to settle into bed.

"You're all right," she said. "You *are* lying down."

He thanked her, and she got back into bed herself. But in a few minutes Dorothy woke again—to the sound of Joseph's last rasping breaths. She called to Kathleen, who was sleeping in the next room.

"Come quickly!" Dorothy cried. "Oh, my God! I think he's going. He can't be—is he?"

Kathleen checked her father's pulse and hugged her mother.

"He's gone, Mom," she said. They sat beside him on the bed, arms around each other.

"How could I have slept when he was dying?" Dorothy asked. "I'd have sat with him all night if I'd known."

"I know you would have, Mom, but he knew you were right there in the bed next to him," Kathleen said. "You know he'd have worried about you if you'd sat up all night. He never did like a fuss."

Mother and daughter sat in silence as the dawn's light rose in the room, catching the bright yellow bindings of the *National Geographic*s arranged on the bookshelves.

"I've been thinking about what Dad said to me last night," Kathleen said. "When he was saying, 'Now I can lie down,' he wasn't talking about taking a rest, he was talking about letting go. He wanted me here in the house so you wouldn't be alone when he died. And he died the way he lived: he was quiet and peaceful and he protected us both in his dying as he did in his living. It was the last thing he could do to take care of us."

At her father's funeral, Kathleen told a coworker about the irony of her reaction to his last comments. She remarked on the ease with which she'd become enmeshed in the web of pain, conflict, and assumption that can confuse those taking care of a dying person they love, causing her to miss her father's real message, even though she was a seasoned health professional.

"If one of my patients had said, 'Now I can lie down,' I probably would have realized in a second what he really meant, but because it was coming from my own father, I missed the message," she said. "But at least I was there, and by being there I might have given him the chance to let go in peace, knowing that I was on hand to help my mother."

• • •

Joseph waited for his daughter, who he knew would provide the support his wife needed when he died. Sometimes people wait for some other reason: perhaps a grandchild's birth, or a son's graduation, or a family member or friend who needs to say good-bye.

HAZEL

Hazel was dying of ovarian cancer. She had three daughters. Debbie, the oldest, was married and lived a few miles away; Susie, twenty-five, still lived at home. Cindy, the youngest, was described by her parents as "our problem child." She'd left home at eighteen to become an actress, deeply worrying Hazel and her husband, Don. Cindy never wrote, and rarely called. Now and again, she'd come home unannounced for a visit that always ended in the same argument with her mother. Cindy found Hazel domineering and judgmental; Hazel thought Cindy unloving and irresponsible.

"The trouble is, they're too much alike," Don said. "They're both strong, intelligent, loving women, but they're also very bossy. It doesn't bother me or our older daughters, we just let it roll off us, but they really rub each other the wrong way. The worst thing anyone can say to Cindy is she's like her mother; she thinks that a terrible insult."

When the doctors told Hazel she wouldn't live much longer, she and Don told Debbie and Susie, who vowed to help keep Hazel at home as long as possible. When they called Cindy, who was living in New York City, she was tearful but calm—until Don and Hazel asked if she'd come home to live during Hazel's final months.

"Never!" Cindy screamed, slamming down the receiver. A few minutes later she called to say she'd be home soon for a visit.

Cindy came home several times in the next few months, but the time spent with her mother was no better than it had ever been. Counseling helped Hazel deal with the pain of this difficult relationship, but Cindy refused several offers of counseling or support.

Hazel's gradual decline toward death changed one morning when she suddenly developed signs of heart failure. Death seemed imminent. She decided to move into the hospice inpatient unit; while waiting for the ambulance, Don called all three daughters. When they arrived, Debbie and Susie were waiting for them; Cindy wouldn't be able to get there until eleven that night.

Hazel lost consciousness. Her blood pressure was very low; her pulse, very weak; her breathing, almost inaudible. She seemed unlikely to last the afternoon. We urged Don, Debbie, and Susie to keep talking to her, and to tell her that Cindy would be coming. Like most families, after a few "I love you's" and "Thank you's," they didn't know what to say.

"You could reminisce about the experiences you've shared as a family," I suggested. Soon Don and their daughters were sitting on Hazel's bed, telling stories as she lay among the pillows.

Just before 11 P.M., a disheveled Cindy appeared. Her father and sisters greeted her with hugs and kisses, making room for her on the bed near her mother. She kissed Hazel's cheek, held her hand, and sobbed. After a few minutes she asked Susie for tissues, and nodded gratefully when Debbie offered her a cup of tea. She calmed down, listening as Don repeated some of the stories. Cindy had memories of her own, recalling how when her older sisters had left for college each semester Hazel would take her out to lunch.

"I never told her how special that made me feel," Cindy said, sipping her tea. "And I never told her I felt really proud when people said I took after her. I've been so mean to her, and now it's too late to apologize."

"The nurses keep telling us she can probably hear what we're saying," Don said. "She probably heard what you just said, do you want to tell her again?"

Cindy took a deep breath, looked into her mother's face, and repeated what she'd said.

About 2:30 A.M. Hazel's breathing became very irregular. Don and the three sisters snuggled up to her, holding one another and Hazel as she took a few slow breaths, then stopped breathing, her life ending on a note of peace and tranquility.

We don't know that Hazel heard what her husband and daughters told her, or that she waited for Cindy to arrive, or that she held on even longer to give her "problem daughter" a chance to express some of her love and regrets. All we know is that Hazel, who wasn't expected to live through the afternoon, survived until the next morning, during which time Cindy was able to ease some of the pain that surely would have made her grieving more difficult.

There are many stories like Hazel's. One dying woman waited for a daughter to return from Europe. A man waited until his wife returned from a trip to help a sick relative in another part of the country (he said, "She shouldn't have to deal with two crises in two different places at the same time"). But we have also seen people who wait for the people they love to leave.

CATHY

Cathy's story offers another good example of choosing a time to die in order to spare loved ones, but there's also an important message here for nurses and other professional caregivers.

Independent, a gifted dancer and teacher of dance, and an aspiring writer, Cathy had a brain tumor, diagnosed only three months after she married. She and her young husband were devastated and frightened, as were her parents.

Her mother took a leave of absence from her job as a writer and research scientist in the food industry to help with her daughter's care. Cathy's mother had a strong influence on her and their relationship was especially close.

During my first visit Cathy had been very clear that she had important goals to reach—to celebrate her first wedding anniversary, and to finish writing a book comparing the styles of early twentieth-century choreographers. Her research was completed just prior to her illness. She wanted to write a book bringing the excitement and commitment she found in her research on past choreographers like Isadora Duncan to young dancers and lay people.

My heart sank when she said this; these goals seemed impossible, as sick as she was. It was unlikely that Cathy would live for her anniversary six months away, much less have the energy and concentration to write a book. But I have learned that when dying people have important goals more often than not they reach them.

"It's helpful for me to know your goals," I said. "So let's get busy and work together; we've got lots to do."

She smiled.

Cathy's parents had hired private-duty nurses around the clock so her husband could continue working. Bedridden, blind, and unable to do anything for herself, she needed complete care for all her needs, but retained her strong spirit and unpredictable wit. Despite her illness, Cathy's home was often full of laughter and outrageous conspiracies.

Cathy was often sleepy; because of the disease in her brain, when she was awake, her thought processes were fragmented. Yet her mother could sit down by her bed and say, "Cathy, I'm ready to take dictation for your book," and—as if flipping a switch—Cathy would become quite clear dictating her thoughts, helping her mother organize and integrate her research.

"You look like you're getting tired, now," her mother would say. "So let's stop for today."

And Cathy's thought processes and speech would become fragmented, and confusion would swallow her again.

Amazingly, Cathy did finish her manuscript, which was accepted for publication just before her death. Equally amazing, Cathy lived to celebrate her wedding anniversary; it was a wonderful party!

With her goals met, we prepared ourselves for Cathy's death, as everyone had become very attached to her. She was so ill it was difficult to understand what could possibly be keeping her alive. The quality of her life seemed so poor we wondered what was holding her back. It was difficult for all involved to watch.

Her mother was to receive a prestigious award in Europe. Cathy's parents agonized about going, sure she would die while they were gone, and that certainly seemed likely. During one of Cathy's mentally clear times she asked to be involved in that decision.

"I want you to go," she said. "It's important to me that Mom get the award she worked so hard for." Together they decided that it was the right thing to do.

As Cathy's mother had played such a strong role in her life, I wondered if she felt that her mother might hold her back. She'd been a powerful influence on Cathy.

Although it hasn't been our experience with hospice, it's common for dying children to send their parents away so they can die in peace. It's as though they sense their parents could hold them back from dying peacefully, or they wish to spare them the anguish of witnessing their moment of death.

Once Cathy's parents decided to go to Europe, I thought perhaps that was what Cathy needed. It was not enough for Mom not to be in her room, or apartment, or town; she needed to be that far away for Cathy to feel safe enough to go.

Cathy and her parents tearfully said their good-byes. Her mother and father left on their trip. But Cathy didn't die. The nurses tried to figure out what it was that Cathy needed. She was no longer able to tell them herself.

Suddenly, without warning, Cathy quietly died, and it was clear to us. Through the window, the day nurse had seen the evening nurse struggling to carry supplies from her car. She ran out to help, leaving Cathy alone for perhaps three minutes— probably the only time she'd been alone for months. That was the time Cathy chose to leave. Her husband was jogging, her parents were in Europe, and the two nurses away from her bedside.

In retrospect, we realized Cathy's final gift to the people she cared about was sparing them, and showing them her own strength in choosing to die alone.

An important message here to nurses as well as to other health-care personnel is that some patients, despite our insistence that it's not their responsibility, will try to take care of us.

Cathy had grown to love her nurses as they had grown to love her. They did a wonderful job of taking care of her for a long time; and in her dying, she took care of them. They too were loved, cared for, and spared.

Sometimes a dying person is waiting for a particular circumstance or condition, but the person chosen to provide it isn't always family.

JEAN

Jean, a writer, had kept working until two weeks before she was admitted to the hospice program. She was quite clear about her wishes: she wanted no further treatment, nor did she want to return to the hospital. For the time she had left she wanted to be as comfortable as possible, so she could use her time writing and exploring her newly discovered faith in God. And she wanted to die at home.

That was her major concern. Jean feared the impact of her dying at home on her dearest friend, Barbara, with whom she'd shared a home for more than twelve years. Jean feared the memories of her dying might make the house an unbearable place for Barbara, and didn't want Barbara to have to watch her at the moment of her death.

But Barbara insisted that Jean get her wish. Admitting she'd need advice and assistance, she said she'd be able to manage.

The three of us had many conversations about this. I explained that as a person gets closer to death hospice staff usually are able to say, "Sometime in the next few days . . ."

At this point families may need more contact with the hospice team to obtain emotional support and learn additional skills. Hospice nurses usually can teach families any skills needed; some families may choose to hire extra nurses.

Jean and Barbara agreed that as the end neared they would hire nurses to provide twenty-four-hour care so Barbara would have someone with her at all times. Jean asked if I could be the nurse there with Barbara when she died. I couldn't promise that; it seemed more likely that a private-duty nurse would be present when she died.

About six months after being admitted to the hospice program, Jean's deterioration began to accelerate. Soon she couldn't get out of bed, didn't want to eat, had cut her fluid consumption to almost nothing, and was becoming less interested in the outside world.

She became weaker. The nurses bathed her, kept her mouth moist, changed her colostomy bag, and injected her pain medicines. They also turned her from side to side every few hours to keep fluid from collecting in her lungs.

On a Friday, her voice reduced to a whisper, Jean said goodbye to Barbara, her brother, her rabbi, and me. Then she slipped into a coma.

The next morning I dropped in to see how Jean and Barbara were doing. The nurse on duty thought Jean seemed comfortable. Her pain seemed to be under control, her breathing was quiet and easy.

"The hard part is over, Jean," I said, kissing her cheek. "From now on it should be easy. You can go whenever you are ready. I'm just going into the other room to talk with Barbara. I'll be back to see you before I leave."

I left Jean with the other nurse, and went with Barbara into the living room. While we were talking, Jean died—as she had wanted, at home, with Barbara on hand but not present, and with me there for Barbara's support.

My first reaction was guilt: "I should have had Barbara there with her." Of course, what mattered was not what I wanted or what I thought was best, but what Jean wanted, and what she thought would be best for Barbara. Knowing that Barbara would have my presence and support, Jean chose her moment to die.

Sparing those closest from witnessing the dying event, or sparing them the effort of providing the care, seems to underlie many dying people's choice of a particular time to die.

BEATRICE

Beatrice was a woman in her mid-sixties, dying of lymphoma. Her husband had been in poor health himself for many years. He was able to provide a great deal of emotional support, but wasn't able to manage his wife's physical care. Her older sister, Agnes, flew down from Maine to help, but Beatrice was very concerned about this arrangement. Agnes's husband was also in poor health and depended heavily on her.

"I don't know what we will do," Beatrice said. "Agnes should be back home with her husband. I'd feel so responsible if anything happened to him while she was here. She's not young herself, and she's spent her whole life taking care of people. It's just not fair. I'm worried sick about her."

Her disease was extensive, but Beatrice was doing fairly well. With assistance, she was able to be out of bed and dressed every day; she ate well and had no discomfort. She seemed to be deteriorating very slowly. Her doctor felt she certainly would live for weeks, possibly a month or two. But this was not happy news for Beatrice.

"I just want to get this over with," she said. "I don't want it to drag on. It's too much for all of us, especially my sister."

One night I received a call from Beatrice's husband. "Agnes was taken to the hospital with an attack of appendicitis this afternoon," he said. "She's been operated on and is doing well, the doctor reports."

"I'm sorry to hear that," I said. "But I'm glad she's okay. How are you and Beatrice managing?"

"Friends and neighbors are all pitching in and we're really doing fine," he said. "But Bea is very concerned about Agnes."

I offered to arrange some shifts of private-duty nurses, but he refused.

"Let's leave things the way they are for now; we're dealing with enough change as it is," he said. "Getting used to strangers may upset Bea even more."

I suggested we talk with Beatrice about it when I visited in three days.

I was shocked the next morning by a frantic call from the neighbor who had spent the night in Beatrice's home. She'd found Beatrice dead in the morning; as far as she could tell, Beatrice had died peacefully in her sleep. I asked her to review the events of the night.

"Everything seemed fine," she said. "Bea kept talking about how worried she was about her sister. But she had a good dinner, took her usual pills, and went to sleep. I peeked in a few times, and she seemed to be sleeping soundly. I'm a light sleeper and was right in the next room. But I didn't hear a thing. I can't believe this."

When I arrived at the house, Beatrice's husband tearfully handed me a note he'd found on her bedside table.

"Don't forget to help Agnes make her plane reservations," it read.

"I wonder when she wrote this?" he said, shaking his head.

Beatrice seemed to have chosen a time to die that spared everyone. Her husband wasn't alone—the neighbor was there—and her sister was safe, receiving good care in the hospital. By dying when she did, her sister was prevented from having to continue caring for her. Coincidence? Perhaps. Or did Beatrice give a final, loving gift of sparing to the people she loved?

For some people, the special conditions needed for them to die may mean the location.

LOUISE

Quiet, regal, and sixty, Louise was happy being a wife, mother, and homemaker. Her marriage, grown children, and beautiful home reflected her dedication and investment of time and love. Her life was a success in every way.

Richard was due to retire, so he and Louise sold their large home and bought a condominium in an expensive part of the city. In a way, it was like starting over—no children, an empty living space, and the challenge of making a nest out of bare walls and floors.

Louise threw herself into decorating with great enthusiasm and attention to detail. Though she was not quite finished, what she had accomplished so far could have graced the pages of the finest decorating magazine. It was breathtaking!

When Louise started to complain of feeling fatigued, Richard urged her to slow down a bit and take it easy. She did, but felt no improvement, so he took her to the family doctor for a checkup. The doctor called within hours of seeing her.

"Louise has a serious problem with her blood counts," he said. "You must take her to the hospital right away, I'll meet you there!" Further tests confirmed his dreaded suspicion: Louise had acute leukemia. She was admitted to the hospital.

The chemotherapy was grueling, but Louise accepted it with the same quiet, regal manner that was so much a part of her style. But often she said to Richard, "I just want to be in my own bed, in my own room."

But each time she seemed to improve enough to be discharged, a complication would develop, and sending her home would again be postponed.

Louise asked Richard to bring her pictures of each room in the condo, so she could show the nurses and "so I won't forget where I left off with the decorating," she explained.

Her daughter brought fabric and wallpaper samples for her to look at. But soon she became weaker, and even these small pleasures became too difficult to manage.

The doctor told Richard and Louise that she was not responding to treatment. To continue them could cause her death, as she was deteriorating so rapidly.

Tearfully Richard and the children discussed the situation with Louise.

"Take me home," she said. "I want to be in my own bed, in my beautiful home."

Richard asked hospice to help him prepare for Louise's homecoming, requesting that the nurse be at their home before the ambulance arrived to make sure everything was ready. The private-duty nurse and I arrived the next day, well before the appointed hour. After looking around, we reassured Richard that he'd done a fine job of preparing for Louise's homecoming. Everything was in order, right down to her favorite ice cream in the freezer. He was nervous, but relieved.

"Everything's got to be just perfect for her," he said.

The ambulance attendants carried Louise off the elevator and in through the apartment door. Her eyes were bright; she was smiling radiantly as she looked around.

"Would you mind carrying me into the living room?" she softly asked the attendants. "If I could just have a moment there." They smiled and nodded. "And now the dining room?" she asked timidly. Then the kitchen, the library, the balcony, the den, and each of the bedrooms received Louise's scrutiny. Richard had put flower arrangements in each room especially for Louise's homecoming. She was delighted. She finally was put into her own bed with a sigh of pure contentment.

"Richard, my dear," she said, "Thank you so very much. Everything looks just beautiful!" She held his hand to her cheek and kissed it.

The private-duty nurse sat with Louise as Richard and I went into the kitchen to finish getting necessary information. Within moments the nurse rushed in.

"Come quickly," she said. "I think she's dying."

By the time the three of us reached the bedroom, Louise had died—a radiant smile still on her face.

Perhaps some might think Louise would have died at that particular moment regardless of the circumstances; certainly, she was desperately ill. But we feel Louise knew she was dying, was very clear about her desire to be in her beautiful home again, and having accomplished that, chose just the right time to die quietly and peacefully.

JUDY

Judy, seventeen, had leukemia. She wanted badly to finish high school but realized she'd probably die before graduation. Her parents, John and Marion, urged her to keep fighting.

One evening John called me; Judy had asked how much time usually passed between the time someone died and the funeral. He and his wife had evaded the question, not wanting to encourage morbid thoughts.

"I guess we could've told her, but we didn't think that was right," John said. "Why do you suppose she wanted to know that?"

I suggested they tell Judy the truth, then ask her gently why she wanted to know.

"Keep an open mind," I said. "Try to respond as best you can."

Apologizing to Judy for avoiding her question, John explained that funerals usually take place two or three days after someone dies.

"Why did you want to know?" her mother asked.

"I didn't want to cause a problem at school," Judy said. "Everybody is up to their ears with studying and college applications, and I know if my funeral is in the middle of the week they'll all be too upset to concentrate. So I guess a Friday would be best. They could find out after school, and you'd have all day Saturday to get the relatives together. We could have the funeral on Sunday and my friends wouldn't have to miss any school."

That night John described this conversation to me. I asked how he felt about what Judy had said.

"Well, Marion and I couldn't believe how calmly Judy talked about dying and having a funeral," he said. "She didn't seem upset at all. Why is that?"

I suggested that it probably meant Judy was comfortable with the idea of dying, and that it was quite possible that she could control the timing of her death so it would occur on a Friday.

"How does your church feel about funerals on Sunday?'" I asked.

"I don't remember one on Sunday before," John said. "Do

you think I should ask the minister or will she think I'm crazy?"

I encouraged John to discuss the matter with the minister, who said she'd help in whatever way she could, including a Sunday funeral if that's what Judy wanted.

It was no surprise when, several weeks later, Judy died shortly after noon on a Friday. The principal held an assembly for the seniors, and told them Judy had died. The weekend went smoothly, following the schedule she had planned. John and Marion seemed to have been able to absorb their daughter's calm attitude about dying, and they took pride in her concern for those around her.

All of us have significant dates—birthdays, anniversaries, holidays. Dying people often try to wait for an important date to pass before dying, so as not to spoil it for the family.

A L

Al was a tough fifty-year-old who'd fought his way through life—it showed in his weary eyes and scarred body. He was a laborer. Crystal, a hardware-store clerk and waitress he'd married four years before, liked to match him drink for drink and egg him into showing off the tattoos that dated back to his Navy days.

She, too, showed signs of a difficult life—broken marriages, the strain of raising children alone, a life on the brink of poverty. But somehow they'd found each other, lived together, and finally married. They were happy, inseparable, and proud of the few possessions they had in their small apartment.

Al worked as long as he could, through the many surgeries and treatments for his kidney cancer. The increasing weakness and weight loss changed him into a shadow of the robust man he had once been. On disability, he constantly worried how they would manage with the cut in pay and increasing medical bills. Crystal would wrap her plump arms around him.

"Never you mind, baby!" she'd say. "As long as you got Crystal, you got everything you need."

She worked forty hours a week as a store clerk and another twenty waitressing in an all-night diner. They needed the money but she worried about leaving Al alone. One day, to her horror, she found Al on the floor when she came home from work: he'd slipped off the couch, and was too weak to get up, and so lay waiting for her to come home.

"That's it!" she said, and quit both jobs. Adamantly, she refused extra nursing assistance and offers of help from friends and relatives.

"He's my man," Crystal said. "I'll do for him! We'll worry about the money later. He needs me now!"

To bring in money, she took in laundry and provided day care in their apartment for neighbors' children, before and after school. Despite their overwhelming problems, Al and Crystal were happy and grew even closer.

Two weeks before Christmas, Al fell again, breaking his hip. Crystal moved into the chair by the side of his bed in the hospital. I urged her to go home at night; I was concerned she'd become exhausted sleeping in the hospital chair.

"Honey, don't you fret!" she said, laughing. "I'm sleeping just fine. I got pillows everywhere!" She patted her round body. She gestured for me to go out in the hall with her.

"I feel like he's slipping away from me," she said, with tears welling up in her eyes. "He sleeps all the time and won't eat. Sometimes he talks out of his head. He keeps saying, 'I can't spoil it, I can't spoil it.' I don't know what he's talking about. He thinks he's at home and keeps asking me if Christmas is over yet; I'm taking him home. That's all I got to say about it!"

I suggested to her that Al might be close to dying and telling her he was worried that this would spoil Christmas for her now and in the future, because of sad memories. Her eyes became large and she marched back into his room.

"Listen here, Al," she said firmly. "There ain't *nothing* you could *ever* do to spoil *anything* for me. I love you. We're going home and I'm going to take care of you, y'hear?"

Al smiled and nodded.

The ambulance brought him home to a festive scene—music, lights, streamers, and decorations everywhere! Crystal was wearing her finest dress and Christmas-tree earrings. In the center of the living room stood a rented hospital bed, full of gifts. Al's eyes were wide as a child's. On the night of the 26th, he died peacefully, wearing some of his Christmas gifts from Crystal—a T-shirt declaring "HANDS OFF! HE'S MINE!" and a new imitation gold chain around his neck. As at the hospital, Crystal had slept alongside him in a chair, with her head resting on the bed by his hand.

"I know it sounds crazy," she said at the funeral, "but it was the best Christmas. He was worried about spoiling it for me, but he knew I loved to fuss over him, so that fussing was like giving him presents. It made this Christmas real special for me. I'll never forget that!"

Al's words "I can't spoil it!" and frequent questions about Christmas helped Crystal see his distress and do what she could to ease it, giving him the permission and reassurance he needed so badly.

Sometimes the right circumstances include receiving permission to die from another person. Permission may be given indirectly— "Everything will be fine"—or more specifically—"Just let go. I'll miss you, but I know you need to go now." With some people permission needs to be very clear, and very direct.

BERNIE

Greer was my college roommate, and we've remained best friends since our nursing-school days twenty-five years ago. Our long-distance phone bills have always been large but increased significantly when her favorite uncle, Bernie, was diagnosed with advanced colon cancer.

Bernie was a man who played by the rules, inclined to dot the i's and cross the t's; he lived by the letter of the law. He'd been the family patriarch since the death of Greer's father and remained so despite his deteriorating condition. At eighty-nine, he insisted on living alone. His wife had died years before; they'd had no children. Greer's family supported his desire for independence, but worried about his well-being.

However, two of Bernie's neighbors came by every evening to fix dinner and visit with him. When they called Greer to report his rapidly increasing weakness and physical changes, she planned a visit.

When she saw him, her heart sank. Six feet tall, Bernie now weighed only one hundred pounds. He couldn't get out of the chair without help. His doctor agreed he needed terminal care; the local hospice responded quickly, admitting him to its home-care program the day after she called.

To complement the hospice staff, his neighbors offered to move in with Bernie and provide him the care he needed, with some additional nursing help hired by the family. Greer's brother, who lived an hour away, visited regularly, as he had been doing for months. Relieved that Bernie had the help he needed, Greer felt comfortable enough to return home.

Six weeks later, the hospice nurse called. Bernie was slipping in and out of a coma; he might die in a day or two. Greer, her mother—dubbed "Sis" by Bernie—and her brother returned to be with him. He rallied for a few days, energized by his role as "host" for this family gathering, but then weakened to the point of being bedridden and barely able to swallow or talk.

They knew he would die soon and were grateful that he seemed so comfortable, but it was a sad and difficult time. Hearing the stress in my friend's voice over the phone I offered to drive up and help them care for Bernie.

"That would be great," she said. "This is so much harder than Mom or I thought it would be." To monitor Bernie during brief periods when no one was with him, Greer set up an intercom by his bed, keeping the speaker with us when we were elsewhere in the house.

"Sis, I've got to go home," Bernie told Greer's mother.

"I know you do," she said. "It's okay. We're ready for you to go. A lot of people we love are waiting for you there. You just go ahead whenever you're ready."

He smiled. "Sis, I want you to come with me," he said.

"Bernie, I can't go just yet, but you tell everybody there that I'll be along soon."

"Okay," he said, smiling weakly. Two days later he stopped being able to talk, but began reaching and waving with an urgent expression. Greer's Mom sat with him for hours, talking of relatives who'd already died and probably were waiting for him: his wife, her brother, grandparents.

He looked at her with surprise. "They're right there!" he said clearly. He never talked again, but continued reaching and waving all night.

At dawn he drifted into a coma, but seemed to be lingering. We wondered if something was keeping him back. The stress of this was beginning to affect everyone; tempers were short and tears were close. Greer prayed that Bernie would be able to go soon. She wanted his dying to be peaceful for him and for her family. We had taken turns spending the night with Bernie and this night it was Greer's Mom's turn. But we were all restless, drifting in and out of his room. At 3 A.M. Greer and I sat together for a moment in the family room. We were startled by her Mom's stage whisper over the intercom.

"Bernie, listen to me," she said. "It's Sis. This is important! Your work here is done, so tonight's the night to go. Do you hear me? It's Sis—telling you that it's okay to go tonight."

Within minutes, Greer looked at me in amazement. "Do you hear how his breathing just changed?" she said. "Can you believe it?"

We were all around his bed when he died quietly at 7 A.M. We praised Greer's Mom for the way she'd spoken to Bernie. She was embarrassed that we'd heard her.

"I don't want you to think I was rushing him," she said. "I just felt that his reaching and waving meant he was struggling with the decision to go or not, and that's why he was lingering so."

We've since chuckled about how closely Bernie's precision carried through in his dying. We'd told him what we thought about where he was going, who we thought would be there for him, and that everyone was ready for him to go. But none of

us, except Greer's Mom, thought to tell him when to go. That
was the missing piece. That's what he needed.

When we give presentations on the materials in this book, we
find this theme affects people in a very powerful way. Often
someone will say, "Now I understand something that has been
bothering me for many years." They go on to tell us a story that
goes something like this:

"Ten years ago, my husband/mother/child was very sick in
the hospital. I'd been there continuously for a week. One evening she/he said, 'You go home tonight and get some rest.' So
I went home at ten o'clock and she/he died at midnight. All
these years I've felt guilty that I wasn't there; but now I'm
wondering if maybe she/he wanted it that way?"

With prompting, people often can figure out such a decision.
"Well, he was always a very private person; it's not surprising
he'd want to die alone" or "Mother always wanted to protect us
from her suffering. I guess she thought it would be easier for
us if we weren't there at the end."

Most people believe that we die when "our time is up," or
when an illness finally overcomes the body; they see death as
passive and the dying person as powerless. In fact, many people
are able to exercise some control over their deaths; knowing
about that control—of the time, the circumstances, and the
people present—makes dying seem less passive and helps show
that dying people do have power.

CHAPTER SIXTEEN

NEARING DEATH

AWARENESS:

PRACTICAL USES

What does it all mean? How do the messages of Nearing Death Awareness and the dynamics that arise around a dying person you may be involved with figure into your life, whether now or in the future?

Begin with some self-examination. In dealing with difficult situations on your own or with others, how do you usually respond to stress? What are your strengths and weaknesses? How will those responses work with someone who is dying? Are you afraid of death? If so, do you know why? Have you had bad personal experiences or are your fears outgrowths of the over-dramatized and often violent portrayal of death depicted on television or in film? Are you afraid of dealing with the unknown?

Most important, what do you expect to accomplish through your involvement with a dying person? Are you acting out of a sense of obligation, to seek fulfillment, or for what reason? Do you want to come away from this death with the sense of completion that accompanies the knowledge that you've done everything you could for the dying person? Is your goal a reconciliation with the one dying? Are you intent on using whatever time remains to savor this relationship? Do you wish to convey important messages of love, gratitude, and farewell? Do you want to learn something that will help you face your own mortality?

Take an inventory of your emotions: If you're angry that

someone close to you is dying, can you find the exact source of that anger? What can you do to alleviate it? If you're nervous about being with a dying person, try to identify the basis of your fears. Is it having to face death? Worry about what to say, what to do? Discomfort at showing your sadness with tears? Are sadness and depression immobilizing you into making no response at all? By staying away, are you attempting to avoid the reality of what's happening? Will ignoring the truth make it go away?

Dealing with dying is hard work—physically and mentally— and it's very easy to slip into a frantic outlook that leaves you emotionally depleted, physically exhausted, and utterly overwhelmed.

You'll do a better job if you take care of yourself. Let others share the burdens and responsibilities, as well as the small victories and large sadnesses. Get plenty of rest. Eat well. Exercise regularly. Spend some time each day doing whatever relaxes you. It is important to get out of the house on a regular basis for something other than chores. Go to a movie, concert, or play. Enjoy eating out with a supportive friend. Consider attending meetings of support groups for others in your situation. Try relaxation techniques—music, meditation, imagery, prayer. Seek counseling if needed.

After conducting a personal inventory, look around you. Will you reach out to others for the help you may need?

Are people available to give emotional support during this difficult period? To whom can you safely vent your feelings of anguish and frustration—a family member, friend, or therapist?

Are you confident in the medical professionals involved? Do they seem willing to answer your questions and to give you information and suggestions on how to handle this situation, both practically and emotionally?

Do you have enough assistance with the practical aspects of providing care to the dying person? If not, where and from whom can you get such assistance? What about the day-to-day matters of living and dying—health-insurance coverage, wills, durable powers of attorney, paying the bills, transferring property titles and business holdings?

Having analyzed your intents and coping skills, your goals

and resources, examine those of the other people involved, including the dying person. How will each participant's usual behavior, responses, and goals mesh or clash with your own? How will all these reverberations affect everyone? What impact will they have on the sense of teamwork so necessary in caring for a dying person?

Recall the emotional stages of dealing with death—denial, anger, bargaining, depression, acceptance—and remember that these feelings arise as the dying person and others involved struggle to come to terms with the reality of the diagnosis, adjusting to life with this illness, and preparing for approaching death.

The earlier you can ask and answer all these questions, the easier it will be to prepare for the changes that occur—not only in the dying person's behavior and outlook, but in your own feelings and interactions with others. Remember that needs change, so try to be flexible.

There are a few specific reminders that will help you recognize, understand, and respond to Nearing Death Awareness:

- Pay attention to *everything* the dying person says. You might want to keep pens and a spiral notebook beside the bed so that anyone can jot down notes about gestures, conversations, or anything out of the ordinary said by the dying person. Talk with one another about these comments and gestures.
- Remember that there may be important messages in *any* communication, however vague or garbled. Not every statement made by a dying person has significance, but heed them all so as not to miss the ones that do.
- Watch for key signs: a glassy-eyed look; the appearance of staring through you; distractedness or secretiveness; seemingly inappropriate smiles or gestures, such as pointing, reaching toward someone or something unseen, or waving when no one is there; efforts to pick at the covers or get out of bed for no apparent reason; agitation or distress at your inability to comprehend something the dying person has tried to say.

- Respond to anything you don't understand with gentle inquiries. "Can you tell me what's happening?" is sometimes a helpful way to initiate this kind of conversation. You might also try saying, "You seem different today. Can you tell me why?"
- Pose questions in open-ended, encouraging terms. For example, if a dying person whose mother is long dead says, "My mother's waiting for me," turn that comment into a question: "Mother's waiting for you?" or "I'm so glad she's close to you. Can you tell me about it?"
- Accept and validate what the dying person tells you. If he says, "I see a beautiful place!" say, "That's wonderful! Can you tell me more about it?" or "I'm so pleased. I can see that it makes you happy," or "I'm so glad you're telling me this. I really want to understand what's happening to you. Can you tell me more?"
- Don't argue or challenge. By saying something like "You couldn't possibly have seen Mother, she's been dead for ten years," you could increase the dying person's frustration and isolation, and run the risk of putting an end to further attempts at communicating.
- Remember that a dying person may employ images from life experiences like work or hobbies. A pilot may talk about getting ready to go for a flight; carry the metaphor forward: "Do you know when it leaves?" or "Is there anyone on the plane you know?" or "Is there anything I can do to help you get ready for takeoff?"
- Be honest about having trouble understanding. One way is to say, "I think you're trying to tell me something important and I'm trying very hard, but I'm just not getting it. I'll keep on trying. Please don't give up on me."
- Don't push. Let the dying control the breadth and depth of the conversation—they may not be able to put their experiences into words; insisting on more talk may frustrate or overwhelm them.
- Avoid instilling a sense of failure in the dying person. If the information is garbled or the delivery impossibly vague, show that you appreciate the effort by saying, "I can see

that this is hard for you; I appreciate your trying to share it with me," or "I can see you're getting tired/angry/frustrated. Would it be easier if we talked about this later?" or "Don't worry. We'll keep trying and maybe it will come."

- If you don't know what to say, don't say anything. Sometimes the best response is simply to touch the dying person's hand, or smile and stroke his or her forehead. Touching gives the very important message "I'm with you." Or you could say, "That's interesting, let me think about it."
- Remember that sometimes the one dying picks an unlikely confidant. Dying people often try to communicate important information to someone who makes them feel safe—who won't get upset or be taken aback by such confidences. If you're an outsider chosen for this role, share the information as gently and completely as possible with the appropriate family members or friends. They may be more familiar with innuendos in a message because they know the person well.

If you're getting messages that fit into the category of "What I Am Experiencing," they may let you know that the dying person isn't alone, is getting ready to go to another place, is comforted by seeing where he's going, and may know when he will go there. As this awareness increases, a dying person's anxieties and fears evolve into comfort and peace—a transformation that can transform those who witness it, as well.

If you're hearing messages in the category of "What I Need to Die Peacefully," you're being asked to play a significant part. If appropriate, mention the request to others who can help. Let the person know you recognize the importance of what he's asking, that you're working diligently, and give frequent updates on your progress. If you can't fulfill the request, be honest, and offer empathy for this disappointment.

If you find yourself figuring in messages about "Choosing a Time," understand that if the dying person wants you there when death comes, you probably will be there; if he doesn't, you probably won't. So keep going about the business of living without worrying about whether you'll be there or not, and don't feel that you've failed if you aren't there when it happens.

Recognize it as the dying person's choice and possibly a gift of sparing you.

If a dying person conveys the message of needing a spiritual, personal, or moral reconciliation, do whatever you can to see that the issue is resolved. Explain to the person that you're working on it, and describe what you're doing to help move matters along. If things don't work out, gently but honestly explain your lack of success.

If you're hearing messages on the theme of "Being Held Back," review all the categories and earlier communications to see if you can find the missing element. Explain to the one dying that you're trying to understand and provide what's needed.

When a dying person is well enough to talk about symbolic dreams, death generally isn't imminent. Dream interpretation isn't easy. Ask the dying what *they* think the dream means. Think about the mood and feelings reflected in the dream. Does it make the dying person seem frightened, lonely, lost, anxious? Talk with the person, share your thoughts. You could say, "It sounds to me as if you were afraid in that dream," or "Is something frightening you?" Identifying the feelings behind the dream may help the dying person realize what he needs.

For Professional Caregivers

Professional caregivers—doctors, nurses, social workers, clergy, and others involved on a regular basis with the dying— may benefit from the following suggestions.

- Be receptive and open to Nearing Death Awareness, which isn't peculiar to hospice but can occur in any setting— hospital, home care, nursing home, emergency room, intensive or coronary care unit, pediatrics—anywhere people are dying.
- Talk about Nearing Death Awareness with coworkers. Chart such phenomena on patients' records. In reviewing the charts of the patients we have written about, we found that few staff members were charting this important information, even though it left a lasting impression on them.

"It was easy to remember those experiences," one nurse said. "I had a sense that something unusual was happening. I didn't put it on the chart because I didn't want to seem weird or silly to my coworkers."

This innocent conspiracy of silence prevents other professional caregivers from learning of—and being able to respond to—the important needs of the dying person.

- Recognize the differences that distinguish Nearing Death Awareness from near-death experiences. Patients with Nearing Death Awareness are *not* clinically dead, often have such experiences over time and in a more gradual way, and usually can talk *during* the experiences, making them able to share these insights with others. You can help them in their struggles to share this information, and can learn from them as well.

- Most important, don't give in to the understandable temptation to be in the middle of this exciting communication. It's neither your right nor your honor. Your role is to *teach* friends and family members how to listen, understand, and respond appropriately to a dying person's messages. In sharing these communications, they may be able to participate in this negative life event in a positive way, achieve some measure of comfort now and in the future, and perhaps find new meaning in life as well as in death.

What we learn from Nearing Death Awareness isn't a touchstone that will ease every death, nor is it a universal cure for the grief and pain that death brings. However, the messages of Nearing Death Awareness do provide a framework within which death can cease to be viewed as a lonely, frightening, overpowering event, as well as a setting in which those close to the one dying can foster sources of comfort in the face of death's inevitability.

We hope our explanation of Nearing Death Awareness, along with the stories we've told to illustrate our points, have helped you to see dying people as we do—not as mute unfortunates, but as teachers; not shadowy figures, but beacons; not objects of pity and scorn, but individual people with the capacity to illuminate whatever exists beyond this life.

We feel privileged to have known these people and their families, to have cared for them, and to have been of some comfort to them. Our lives have been changed by what they have taught us. This book is our memorial to all of them.

> Life is eternal; and love is immortal; and death is only a horizon; and a horizon is nothing save the limit of our sight.
>
> ROSSITER WORTHINGTON RAYMOND
> *1840–1918*

RECOMMENDED READING

There are numerous books about death and dying available today. The following are particularly useful for those starting to explore the topic of death, and the many issues, questions, and feelings associated with it. This is not a complete bibliography, nor even a list of all the books we have read, appreciated, and learned from. Most of the following books have bibliographies if you wish to explore further any specific area.

About Death
Grollman, Earl A. *Talking About Death*. Boston: Beacon Press, 1970. Helpful suggestions for a difficult topic.
Kübler-Ross, Elisabeth. *On Death and Dying*. New York: Macmillan, 1969.
————. *Questions and Answers on Death and Dying*. New York: Macmillan, 1974. Most people find Dr. Kübler-Ross's books helpful; these earlier books are valuable sources of information about people's reactions to dying.

Information for Children
Buscaglia, Leo. *The Fall of Freddie the Leaf*. New York: Henry Holt, 1982. For children of all ages. Many adults have found this helpful.
Stein, Sara Bonnett. *About Dying*. New York: Walker and Company,

1974. With photographs and a large-print text for children and additional details for parents.

Information for Adolescents
Le Shan, Eda. *When a Parent Is Very Sick.* Boston: Little, Brown, 1986.
————. *Learning to Say Goodbye.* New York: Macmillan, 1976. Both of these are informative, easily read, and helpful to many adults also.

About Dying Children
Kübler-Ross, Elisabeth. *Living with Death and Dying.* New York: Macmillan, 1981. In this book Dr. Kübler-Ross discusses dying children and their families.

About Grief
Kushner, Harold. *When Bad Things Happen to Good People.* New York: Avon Books, 1983. This book brings comfort for times when bad things happen.
Tatelbaum, Judy. *The Courage to Grieve.* New York: Harper & Row, 1982. Helpful when you or someone you love is grieving.
Viorst, Judith. *Necessary Losses.* New York: Ballantine Books, 1986. Information about effects of grief and loss throughout life.
Westberg, Granger. *Good Grief.* Philadelphia: Fortress Press, 1962.

About Hospice
Stoddard, Sandol. *The Hospice Movement.* New York: Vintage Books, 1978. Covers the evolution of the modern hospice movement from its medieval predecessors, and describes how hospice programs work. An updated edition is due out in January 1992.
For information about hospice programs in the United States, contact:
National Hospice Organization
1901 North Moore Street, Suite 901
Arlington, VA 22209
(703) 243-5900

Historical and Contemporary Perspectives on Death
Aries, Phillipe. *The Hour of Our Death.* New York: Alfred A. Knopf, 1981. Covers Western attitudes toward death and dying since the Middle Ages.

Freemantle, Francesca, and Trungpa, Chogyam. *The Tibetan Book of the Dead*. Boston and London, Shambhala Publications, 1975. A translation and commentary on the Buddhist teachings about death and what follows.

Grosz, Anton. *Letters to a Dying Friend*. Wheaton, Illinois, Quest Books, 1989. This is a simple, beautiful presentation of the teachings found in the Tibetan Book of the Dead.

Kübler-Ross, Elisabeth, ed. *Death: The Final Stage of Growth*. New Jersey: Prentice-Hall, 1975. A collection of essays about death from people of different cultures and experiences.

Levine, Stephen. *Who Dies? An Investigation into Conscious Living and Conscious Dying*. New York: Doubleday, 1982. Explores many death-related topics in a thoughtful and thought-provoking way.

Moody, Raymond. *Life after Life*. New York: Bantam Books, 1975. Descriptions and explanations of near-death experiences.

Osis, Karlis, and Haraldsson, Erlendur. *At the Hour of Death*. New York: Avon Publishers, 1977. Similarities in deathbed visions in different cultures.

Ring, Kenneth. *Heading Toward Omega*. New York: William Morrow, 1984. Explores the effects on behavior and values of those who have had near-death experiences.